New Hampshire Beautiful

New Hampshire Beautiful

BY
WALLACE NUTTING

ILLUSTRATED BY THE AUTHOR WITH THREE
HUNDRED AND FOUR PICTURES COVERING
ALL THE COUNTIES IN NEW HAMPSHIRE

BONANZA BOOKS · NEW YORK

FOREWORD

THE state of New Hampshire is better known than any other by the nation of tourists at large. For this reason the numerous pictures, in a form to preserve, of the various portions of the state, will be the more valued by the public. The writer has an affection for New Hampshire, as he passed years of preparation there at Phillips Exeter Academy. It was in that state that he recovered and restored the famous Wentworth-Gardner House, which has now become the property of the Metropolitan Museum.

This book is the fourth in the series on the States Beautiful. At the risk of showing a few pictures, the equivalents of which may perhaps have been made by others, we can but feel that various quarters of the state have been neglected. The writer has made all the pictures himself and has written the bulk of the text, but here and there a poem has been added with the name of its author attached.

It is a dangerous thing to commend or to fail to commend. Especially in a state that is so largely given up to tourists' resorts, the risk of offending by sins of omission is very great. Please let it be understood that neither this book nor any of the series either directly or indirectly permits any advertising features. If we amplify upon the beauties of a certain district it is merely because we know that district better than some other, or we are more taken with it.

The illustrations are more largely new than in any of this series thus far issued. The great body of them were made in the seasons of 1922 and 1923. Not a few are so fresh that they have actually gone directly, the first time seen, from our hands to those of the printer.

All our view-points are not only partial but necessarily superficial. There is very little of the beauty of any state that any one man may see,

3

and still less that he can record. Nevertheless, to assemble in one volume many scattered observations has its advantages, because it becomes a small storehouse not subject to the fluctuation of fashions. There are quarters of the state that go up and others that go down in the vogue of travelers. We have endeavored to give a fair review of the entire state, based upon the appeals of every part as artistic compositions. We must consider the needs and the local patriotism of the average man in New Hampshire who has tilled his native acres all his life, and who loves the district in which he lives apart from any ebb or flow of summer travel. In this series of books we are always thinking of the dweller on the soil, and the villager who looks out on the same fair landscape that has filled the eye of his fathers at least to the third and fourth generations.

While we are aware that this book will pass largely into the hands of tourists, we feel the obligation and the inclination to record for the native son of New Hampshire the things which his eye loves and which form a part of his daily life. New Hampshire is yet, in some portions, to be settled. There are higher slopes that may repay cultivation but which have been neglected by the westward trend of immigration.

We have always had a fondness for seeing the old walls and homesteads set on the slopes of the mountains. With the probably large increase in the number of inhabitants to be looked for in one hundred years in America, many a New Hampshire down and lea and fell will be availed of as a setting for a country home.

The people of New Hampshire possess greater breadth of view and broader sympathy than most other rural people, owing to their contact for generations with the world at large as it comes to visit them. We sincerely hope that this labor of love may have some small influence in enhancing the joy and satisfying the pride of the people of New Hampshire.

WALLACE NUTTING

Framingham, Massachusetts

To

THE NEW HAMPSHIRE HISTORICAL SOCIETY

WHICH HAS IN ITS NOBLE BUILDING IN
CONCORD A NUCLEUS OF VAST VALUE
THIS VOLUME ON THE BEAUTIES OF NEW
HAMPSHIRE IS RESPECTFULLY DEDICATED

New Hampshire Beautiful

• •

NEW HAMPSHIRE

FROM sea beach to mountain top all beautiful! Who does not know her fame for health, rest, and joy! Her head is in the snows and her feet on the ocean marge. She reaches her hands to all the weary children of men. With her is the delight that does not stale. Hers are the surprises which give zest to her acquaintance. New pleasures she offers at every hill-crest, and within her limited bounds she holds scenes mighty to thrall all hearts, whether lovers of stream or lake, valley or hill, soft meadow or solitary summit.

There is more in New Hampshire not yet appropriated than that already known and loved. The undiscovered beauties of her lower plains are little observed. Many a fastness in her secluded hills awaits taming and appreciation. From the quaintness and age of her southern towns to remote upland frontiers of natural untouched grace, she supplies whatever the heart of man may wish to feed upon.

We should cease to go abroad to compare her with other regions. New Hampshire is herself and possesses certain attractions peculiar to her situation, her contour, and her people. Nothing is so short-sighted as to think of any American district as a substitute or imitation or rival to the attractions of another country. New Hampshire's future lies with herself, her winning qualities and her merits are exclusively her own. In developing them along natural lines, following her own genius she

7

will be most successful, most splendid, most worthy. Winnepesaukee has a glinting grace, a rambling play of water-fingers, a sunlit glory all her own. Each lake, Squam and New Found and Ossipee, has an individuality of charm which endears it most to those who know it best. About Chocorua are springing slopes and nestling waters so fair as to hold perpetually the first place in the hearts of her understanding worshipers.

It is not Washington alone, in singular dignity and majesty, that holds us all, but many another peak discloses intimate beauties and commands reverence from all, fealty from those most observing.

For every fair turn of cliff, every wooded dell, every dimpled elbow of brook, every sparkling expanse, every green solitude, are set forth to catch human sympathy and appreciation. They have waited what aeons of time for us to rejoice in their gorgeousness, and many of them are waiting yet, till a thinking, loving, watching person shall follow their curves and caress their surfaces with the eye of understanding. Nature has yet to be unveiled. Like a rural maiden whose perfections the world does not know, there are landscapes, bowers, dells, becks and burns, there are brows and bosoms of nobility and purity awaiting the awakening of men of spirit and of fire, who have in them poetry and taste, the knowledge of the beautiful and the passion to record what they so passionately see. There must yet be set forth to the world on grander canvases, canvases blending majesty with witchery, the wonderful in New Hampshire; there must yet come into expression nobler, subtler, more delicate utterances of the messages New Hampshire has latent and waiting when uttered for the world's approval.

It is much to dwell in a state where the tillage of the acres is presided over by mountain grandeur; where the gleaning of the meadows is between the witching curves of limpid waters; where the breath of nature wafted in your window is perfumed with the pines and tempered by mountain flowers.

It is a challenge to man to call out the finer aspects of his nature, when the world around him ever beckons and paints and plays in endless shapes of power and splendor.

To live in New Hampshire and not to breath deeply, think strongly, love truly, is a crime against the landscape. For ever, amid the glories of the outer world, we look for stronger men and fairer women, for growth and power and invention and dignity in the character of the people, and we do not look in vain. Generally hill peoples have been free. Often they have been fair. Generally they have been strong. Sometimes they have been wise and noble. Here let there spring and mature a race girded and fed by the faith and the outstanding merits of the spreading grandeurs around. Here rise Americans free and fair, strong, wise, and noble, — the typical, the ultimate American!

NEW HAMPSHIRE BEAUTIFUL

NEW HAMPSHIRE has many claims of a diverse nature upon our attention, and is not merely a mountain state, as the average traveler thinks of it. The district near its short sea-coast is as old and quaint, practically, as any in America. Portsmouth, Hampton, Exeter, and Dover were settled about the same time as Boston. A second feature of interest in New Hampshire is its numerous lakes, large and small. Winnepesaukee, while no longer fashionable, is just as beautiful as ever, and can scarcely be matched in that regard by any American body of water. In fact, whatever our fear of superlatives, we are willing to say that the great variety of its contour and its extent and its surrounding hills permit it to vie with Lake George. The third, and usually the only particularly considered, feature of New Hampshire is its mountains.

New Hampshire is approached by five main gateways: from the North Shore to Hampton and Portsmouth; from Fitchburg to Marlboro, Dublin, and Keene; from Bellows Falls by the way of Alstead; and from Maine entering from Fryeburg into Conway. A fifth well-known route is up the valley of the Merrimac from Nashua. Of course, one coming from the north might enter by way of Littleton from St. Johnsbury, or by way of Gorham from the Rangeley Lakes.

The state, from its small size and mountain barriers, does not require very much attention on our part to its roads.

Southern New Hampshire, outside of the coastal region, is emphasized for us by the Dublin district and Mount Monadnock. Peterboro and Jaffrey complete the trio of towns which center the visitor's attention. The central portion of the state is dominated by the lake district of Winnepesaukee and Sunapee, the latter more of a resort in these days than the former.

The third district is the White Mountain region proper, and the fourth section is the northern tip including the Dixville resorts. The completion of the road from Winchendon to Keene, Lebanon, and the White Mountains has opened a very charming approach. The traveler is interested by the broad plains about Keene and its splendid pines. He is further delighted by the numerous swift water-glimpses on the way north. The cross-state route from Portsmouth through Exeter to Manchester and Concord is not yet completed, but is thoroughly attractive in many parts.

THE SHORE AND PLAINS DISTRICT

THE route from Portsmouth through Stratham to Exeter is a very characteristic and beautiful agricultural district. The dwellings in New Hampshire average very markedly large. We cannot attribute this wholly to the almost universal boarding-house habit which has transformed many a farm-house into a twenty-room edifice. We find it to be the rule that great, square houses were built after the Revolution for some fifty years. There is no such district in Maine or Vermont. It

A LITTLE RIVER AND MOUNT WASHINGTON

THE TURN HOMEWARD—ALSTEAD

THE DELL ROAD—ALSTEAD

is difficult to account for the amplitude of these dwellings. We must believe that the settlers derived from the coast-towns and from Massachusetts their sense of architectural generosity. The valley of the Merrimac and the plains around Exeter encouraged farming on a large scale. New Hampshire, therefore, is not a state of rural cottages but of solid square dwellings. There is a strong English flavor about the environs of Exeter and Hampton. The dwellings often stand well back with long and sometimes stately approaches.

The remarkable water features between Portsmouth and Dover and Exeter, as the three bounding points, are beautiful to a degree. Great Bay, a body of water that many travelers have never heard of, much less seen, was once of more commercial importance for vessels of a considerable size. The meeting of the waters at Dover Point, and the drive thence into Dover along a nobly-sloping ridge, supplies scenery of a most edifying sort. Fair fields and noble trees and endless reaches of water meet us on every hand. The situation of Dover would have been admirable for the development of a great city. The outlooks, such as that from the Rollins estate and other contiguous summer residences, are unexcelled in their sort.

The ancient houses of Portsmouth are pretty well known, but those of Exeter are of scarcely secondary importance. One of these, indeed, is perhaps as early as any remaining in Portsmouth, and a better house than and of about the period of the Jackson house in Portsmouth. We refer to that where Daniel Webster had a room when at school.

[*Text continued on page* 17.]

SINGING BIRCHES

Written for the picture opposite

Along the banks, amid the rock and vines,
The birches stand in clustered, snowy lines.

They sing of golden arrow-heads that blaze
Against the blue, above the autumn trail,
Sighing and crooning as the south wind sways
The graceful branches, silvery and frail.
They sing of golden arrow-heads that rain
In pelting showers when the north wind blows,
As in the Red-men's day the birchen lane
Was startled from its dream of deep repose.

They whisper legends of the birch canoe
That leaped and darted with the magic words
Of painted, supple warriors who knew
The secrets of the fishes and the birds.
They sing of forest paths and mountain caves
And brilliant feathers of the Mohawk scribe;
Of hidden scrolls of birch, and running braves
Who bore the message to a distant tribe.

They whisper songs of friendly, snowy bark,
Where Brave-Heart dared to carve his sign of love,
As somewhere in the sky a meadow-lark
Sang to its mate through drooping boughs above.
They whisper of the wild heart of a maid
That fluttered, like these bright leaves in the breeze,
When Brave-Heart touched her dusky, beaded braid,
And told his love, beneath the singing trees.

Sing while they sleep, O birch and golden rod!
Sing of the happy hunting grounds and God.

MILDRED HOBBS

BIRCH HILL TOP—MACINDOES

THE MONADNOCK REGION

APPROACHING New Hampshire from the south, the important and in fact the only mountain is Monadnock. Around it various legends have gathered which are pretty well known. Its mass dominates southwestern New Hampshire, and is readily seen from many points of the three adjoining states. We have been fortunate in securing a considerable variety of illustrations of this imposing mass, as over Thorndike Pond from the south, over a reservoir in Jaffrey from the west, and from the corner of an old garden-wall in Jaffrey, from the northwest, and from Dublin on the north. Perhaps Monadnock as seen from Dublin Pond in a proper light is one of the three best mountain and water scenes of New Hampshire, the other two being that of Chocorua from its pond, and Mount Washington from a millpond near the east-side state road.

Monadnock has the advantage among New Hampshire mountains of standing severely alone. One can have an affection for such a mountain as a man loves one wife in a different way from the love he must bear a harem. When we get in the White Mountains proper we are confused in our allegiance.

There is, part way up the summit of Monadnock, a summering place, but in general, around its foot, and at Dublin, a large number of summer visitors have gathered. There are numerous beautiful places built apparently with the main concern of securing a fine outlook of the mountain and the pond, as Dublin Lake is generally called.

One may circle Monadnock and keep on roads of a fine or fair quality all the way, especially in the dry season. We have often thought that a summer headquarters of solid fireproof construction and pleasing design on the summit of a mountain might prove attractive to those who find hot weather especially debilitating. We recommend this project to the enterprising, and would suggest that the summit of Monadnock is a site readily made accessible by a highway such as could be constructed with moderate grades. The Tip Top House on Mount Washington seems not

A DREAMY DOOR, PORTSMOUTH

to be a popular resort, partly because the average summer guest is seeking a husband or a wife or the range of gift-shops.   Nevertheless, we have wondered why a carefully-constructed summer resort, with "every

BIRCHES AT RANDOLPH

DIXVILLE SHADOWS

A PEEP AT MOUNT WASHINGTON

CHERRY MOUNTAIN FROM THE ORCHARD

modern comfort and every ancient charm" might not be made on the summit of Mount Washington. The persons who are willing to "rough it" are of the sort who like to go away alone or with a guide. Hence, a hotel to be attractive at all needs to be of considerable size and to be provided with the luxuries of civilization. Monadnock would be far more accessible to the motorist and possibly might be developed into an all-the-year-'round resort, now that winter sports are so popular. We imagine the Dublin people would not look with favor upon such an enterprise, as they are quite content with their summer homes and the absence of the conventional tripper.

The birches in the region around Monadnock are often very fine. They grow to a great size, and are the main feature of roadside decoration.

The approach to Monadnock through Rindge has now been made rather attractive over routes which were once a byword for poor roads. Rindge has become somewhat of a resort, and a very pleasant one, since it is now so accessible from two quarters by the drives through shady forests.

Jaffrey is deservedly a popular resort, affording in particular fine views of the mountain from the intimate aspects of the west, and more than one vista with water foreground. The height of Monadnock is such that it is friendly rather than awesome, and yet its bulk is sufficiently huge to allow its strength to flow into one whose nervous forces are long depleted by the noise and wear of the cities. Perhaps it has more lovers than any other individual mountain in New England. Once known and once become the companion of a summer, it is seldom forsaken by its votaries.

We are not sufficiently familiar with the literature of mountains to know that justice has ever been done to the contrast between the immovable mass of a mountain and the ceaseless play of motion of the clouds above it. Undoubtedly many have enjoyed to the full this combination of the changeless with the changing, who have never attempted to analyze the sensations they have enjoyed.

There is a sort of coquetry in the play of clouds as they saucily kiss the bosom of the mountain and then sheer aside; and again when they gather at the small focus of its peak and resemble the smoke above a volcano, and again when, shrouding the peak in a dense mystery, they lend themselves to the weird fantasies of poets and romanticists. A mountain of the height of Monadnock is in its way a kind of barometer, as those who are familiar with it can gauge the height of the clouds. Such a mountain has a severe and silent and almost sacred beauty when the sky about it is wholly clear. At such times it suggests the loneliness and retired and cold purity which is not as familiar with humanity as others of its moods.

The play of mackerel clouds high above, or of the cumulus summer masses, or of the denser storm clouds, is of infinite and never-ending interest. We feel in looking at such strong and silent forces as the immovable mountain and the momentarily shifting shapes of clouds a certain sense of intimacy and of importance, as if we were being taken into the councils of the great. It may be only a fancy, but if we hold it, it is nevertheless pleasing. We are present, as it were, at the operations of mighty natural agencies. As untold generations have watched the flame play in the fireplace, so as many generations have watched, and it seems to us with a larger inspiration, the mountain tops. The earliest literature teems with reference to the beholder's joy in those strong sentinels that raise their buttresses to the sky to discover what may be in the lap of the gods. The mountains are the abode of the gods, false and true. It was not without a fine sense of propriety that the ancients attributed the mountain seats to various divinities. Most of all, in the Book of books, the mountain-man Moses is associated with the greatest and most striking peak of that vast region where early human history was formed. It is a true conception of the mountains that they enlarge human thought very much in the same way as does the study of the heavens. Mountain-men and astronomers have been affiliated, since they have so very much in common as to their aspirations and their philosophy. It is perhaps natural that the volcano should be assigned to angry gods, and the highest, most

NESTING TIME—LANCASTER

OUTLOOK—LANCASTER-RANDOLPH

PROFILE IN SUMMER

JUNE SHADOWS—GORHAM

A PORTSMOUTH DOOR

inaccessible peaks assigned to the severer majesties that preside over human destiny.

Nevertheless, the love of mountains is more a love of viewing them than being on them. There are ten thousand who pass admiringly along their bases to one who scales their forbidding crags. It is as well. The mountain was designed to be looked at rather than dwelt upon. It is "the shadow of a great rock in a weary land," yet gives, even more than the sea, a sense of permanence and rest and calm and power. It soothes us by its immense reliability, and throws its protecting shadow over many a disturbed spirit. To those who love to climb it there are reserved special pleasures not known to the valley dwellers. Nevertheless to all it brings its contribution of what each needs most and is able to find in it. In this particular, Monadnock, by its situation, appeals to more people than other mountains because we can flee to it more often. In spite, however, of the fixity of mountains which are not volcanic, they present an amazing number of aspects and speak to us in many tongues. There is, for instance, the differing aspect from the various points of the compass, and the position intermediary, so that the casual beholder does not know the mountain to be the same when viewed from some unfamiliar aspect. There are the differing aspects of winter and summer, of spring and autumn, of sunrise and sunset, of storm and calm, of clear, bitten outline and of a soft and mellow haze. There is as wide a variation in the color. We have the cold grays, the empurpled tints, the pink of the earlier and later hours, and the indescribable various shades that an infinity of atmospheric conditions provides. Then, perhaps, best of all is the effect of shadow supplied by the cloud-play, now revealing with splendid clearness some gorge by a burst of sunshine, and now sending floating masses of shadow across forest and cliff, and now bursting in the terror of thunder-riven storm.

Thus between color and shape and time of day and changing seasons there is a variety so vast and so daintily shaded, one aspect into another, that no one knows a mountain or has seen all its moods.

It is a comfort to look out in the morning and find amidst conflagrations and cataclasms that the old mountain is still there. It is an encouragement to those whose ideals waver to see that the sun never forgets to paint the cloud draperies with beauty, and to show a new fashion every week.

THE MOUNT WASHINGTON TRAIL

THE PROFILE ROAD AND LAKE

MOUNT WASHINGTON APPROACH

THE SIDE ROAD

We are encouraged to believe in man by believing in nature. We are taught again that God reigns and that government still lives. Indeed, perhaps the play of the clouds on the eternal rocks was intended to encourage us to believe that whatever the vagaries of men there is something dependable. The cycles come around again to the era of the Golden Age, and the peace of October and the joy of June. The purposes of the Almighty abide, and the mountains are the witnesses that it is so. They stimulate faith in an age of doubt, and encourage and correct a holier taste in a period of degraded art. They are the drawing and coloring of an unerring hand that knows no failure in taste and no wavering of true lines. They speak as well to the moral as to the aesthetic nature. They are the glory of the strong and the weak. To each they bring a different but to all a consoling message. They speak of that which was and is and is to be. We glory in their mystery and we believe in their prophecy. They lead us to rejoice that there is an increasing purpose that moves not only through human but through geologic history. They are the steps to the stars. They are the pillars of our imagination and the pinacles of our outlook. They can be more to us than they have yet brought to any man, but to the weakest and to the least imaginative they bring much. It is a poor mountain that cannot draw every face within view of it from the clod.

The mountains were not so much thought of or written of in the classic age as amongst the stronger Nordic peoples. The people where mountains are can little understand the awe and the vast delight that come to a dweller on the great plains of the Mississippi, we will say, when these vast upheavals that are left to us from a forgotten age are first brought to view. The plains-dweller sees in the mountains very much more than many who live beneath them. From his unbroken prairie he comes suddenly upon a thing beyond his experience, and he is shocked into seeing and feeling much that may have escaped the familiar resident at the base of the mountains. Thus beauty breaks with freshness upon the vision of a hungry life, and calls out new thoughts and expands for every one the limits of his little universe. For, after all, the bounds of the citizen's thought are rather circumscribed. He is engaged either in politics or in business or in some profession, and the tendency of education and of custom and of economics is too much in a trite circle. The newer and different help that comes from the hills is, therefore, a distinct addition of the highest value. The soul of every man who has not seen a mountain is left poor whatever goods and gear he may have gathered.

THE CHOCORUA REGION

CHOCORUA is another of those mountains that stand so much by themselves as to focus our attention. Its sharply serrated and peculiarly individual outline make it perhaps the most marked feature in the state for getting one's bearings. It has a way, as from Silver Lake, of peeping over the intervening hills, like the call of another world. Its lake is of very great beauty, and reminds one, more than anything else in the East, of the Salton Sea beneath its mountains. Of course the scale of Chocorua is very much smaller, but none-the-less beautiful on that account. Advantage has been taken of view-points of this mountain for summer resorts. One should study the effect produced by such choice of locations here, as giving excellent suggestions for other mountain regions. From whatever quarter Chocorua is approached it speaks from afar, its glorious heights wrestling with the storm or bathed in pink or purple, or still more alluringly half hidden in a diaphanous mist. A lake at the foot of such a mountain is like a mirror in a lady's boudoir. There is always a double beauty. The charm of lake and mountain are not doubled but multiplied many-fold when they are in juxtaposition.

The environs of Chocorua comprise various exquisitely beautiful drives. The wooded approach to Wonalancet from Chocorua Lake, a view of which we present, is one of the most entrancing compositions we have

THE WHITE MOUNTAINS—CARROLL

JUNE BEAUTIFUL—CARROLL

ECHO LAKE—MARGE

BLOSSOM CREST—BETHLEHEM

THE RICHTER DOOR   THE WARNER DOOR

ever discovered. The mountain itself, in its various moods seen over the large or the subordinate lake, affords many aspects of beauty. The highway, immediately skirting the lake, is flanked with fine old evergreens. The birches of this region are often massive and always fine. There is a back-road to the east of the main line which takes one past Silver Lake, and so on into Ossipee. The road is mostly good, and on the short poor stretches is merely sandy. Other little lakes are encountered on the journey with charming mountain surroundings.

Ossipee seems a huge town in area, at least with West Ossipee. About the banks of the lake of the same name are some of the most pleasing visions to be found in the state, several of which we have set forth here. Whittier's famous and charming poem on the Saco River turns aside to mention the "vestal waves of Ossipee." The lake does not lie among mountains as lofty as Chocorua, but from Ossipee there are broad views that cannot fail to appeal strongly. Passing west from Chocorua, either by the Wonalancet road or a little farther south on the cross-cut from Moultonboro and Center Harbor, one skirts for some distance the banks of Bear Camp River, on which a good number of fine compositions showing the mountains are unfolded, and this stream continues beautiful throughout its brief course.

Northward from Chocorua the Conway road is interesting. It becomes increasingly important, however, if one slows down to view the scenery, to pull well out of the highway. We have at last acquired the habit of making no stops unless we can secure a turnout that will permit traffic to ignore us. The highways are now so filled with novices as drivers that the danger is always greater from what others may do than from any errors of an old campaigner with a motor car.

There is a by-road some two or three miles north of Chocorua which followed to the right, for miles, comes to an end, but affords fine prospects, and has been sought as a retreat by some wise persons who have found here almost absolute seclusion and fine outlooks far away from the roar and dust of traffic.

THE CONWAY REGION

YEARS ago the Conways had the preëminence among New Hampshire resorts, and so far as general view of mountain and meadow are concerned we think they still deserve that high place. The Conway meadows at one point or another show more fine horizons, perhaps, than are visible elsewhere in such an extent in New Hampshire.

From the bridge on the back road between Conway and North Conway, and on the way to Echo Lake, there is one of the best compositions we have ever beheld. Echo Lake, with its miniature but peculiarly shaped mountains, is deservedly a much-sought *rendezvous*. Diana's Baths, when we saw them, might possibly have answered as a foot bath for that

CITY OF PARIS PAPER

MOUNTAIN ORCHARD — LANCASTER

THE RANDOLPH STREAM

PLINY RANGE

lady, and if she walked to them she would have needed it. In time of low water their chief attraction is the water-worn rocks, fantastically cut with curious curves into all sorts of forms which the imaginative delight to name after all our presidents and various other worthies. In time of high water, the falls are impressive with their rushing power, and their contour is singularly beautiful.

One of the chief charms of Conway is an excursion on its meadows, as, for instance, from North Conway over the field-roads and little fords, pictorial records of which we have made. It was on an occasion like this that we came upon what is to us the the greatest maple, having a circumference of about twenty feet at the height of the shoulder, which is taken as the waist line of trees. The largest maple we have hitherto come upon was in the town of Lancaster, Massachusetts, with a circumference of fourteen feet. These intervale lands are especially favorable to the huge growths of trees, although in this region the oak seems not prominent, but the elm is present in every aspect of its various graces.

Teeta, when we had wandered some distance from our car, following a stream, volunteered to go back to bring additional photographic plates, as we discovered more beautiful things than we had looked for. By the time she had arrived with the plates, still more exquisite things had been discovered, and she remembers this excursion as one in which she was engaged in a walking tour from stream to car for several hours, each trip being supposed to be the last, until finally we crowned the morning with a catch of twenty stream or pool or mountain pictures. As ever, we proved to ourselves how much a brook surpasses a river in its adaptation to artistic composition. Its border of a series of majestic, companionable trees, its curves over golden sands, its accommodating foreground to compose with a middle distance of majestic elms and background of serrated peaks, its surprises at every turn, its little fords, its long grasses " laved lingeringly " by its musical flow, — all left us an impression of enchantment which will come to us for years as dreams in the night or as sweet recollections at rest times.

It is odd that on a meadow one may see far. In fact, at the center of a considerable meadow, mountains seem more beautiful than from any other view-point. It is here that the Saco, coming down from Crawford's Notch where it begins as a rivulet, spreads into many a pool, and winds in many a curve of beauty.

The Conways afford that unusual combination of village communities with all the conveniences of modern life, and surrounded by fertile lands, yet located in an amphitheatre of bulwarked beauty.

Accessible directly from the most famous inland Maine resorts and the Maine coast as well as from the New Hampshire shore, the Conways must in the long run make good their claim to the lover of the beautiful, who, nevertheless, also loves to dwell with men, amid those small village features so favorable for the development of American character. The highways are largely on the edges of the benches formed by geologic change, so that we pass over comparatively level stretches. We look down to the lower basin and up to the circling-heights, which are here cones, there battlements, and yonder monuments and strange nameless contours that stimulate the imagination by their changing lights.

One feels at Conway something the same sensation as traveling along the crests of the Holy Land. We are in the presence of the whole earth. We appear to be as in a little Greek state in a miniature empire all our own, our harvest fields and lush grasses near at hand, our larger streams which come from the heights and pass us to the sea, and the guarding, beckoning boundaries of beauty in the arching rampart of the hills. We seem here to want nothing beyond what is under our feet and within the scope of our eyes. There is a fair heaven above us, with its flocks of cloud assuming every form except those of ugliness, and revealing every color except gloom. They sail away to overtop or to meet and kiss or veil the neighboring peaks. They disappear and leave an unsoiled azure. They peep again over the most distant ranges. They are always interesting, always mysterious, always beautiful, and always beneficent.

WHITE MOUNTAINS FROM JEFFERSON

THE RANGE FROM RANDOLPH

DOWN FROM MOUNT WASHINGTON

A FRANCONIA BLOSSOM BROOK

JACKSON HOUSE (c. 1660) PORTSMOUTH

One feels in such an empire among the hills that the wealth of waters will never fail him, and the bounty of the earth will be sufficient. The glory of the meadow, of the vale, and of the slope are all ours. The palest green of May, the darkest shades of summer foliage, and the ever-surprising glamour of every golden autumn are ours. From the time when the hills are shrouded in their mantle of white, through the summer solstice to the early winter again, no day is without its new vision and new call to enjoy and to breath deeply and love largely the splendor of this kingdom of beauty and of peace.

When we consider the horrible conditions of human life on many distant shores and alien valleys, where great peaks buttress the sky or historic seas lave the coasts, what a sharp sense of relief it is to come back to our own native domain.

> "*I love thy rocks and rills,*
> *Thy woods and templed hills,*
> *My heart with rapture thrills*
> *Like that above.*"

It is not possible to brush away the fact that the hills help us. They become our peace and their virtue flows into us. They calm our fretfulness and call our spirits up. If the nervous unrest and the long suicide of competition are to be counteracted it must be by retreat into these sanctities unspoiled by bad men and eternally solacing to good men.

To have a home facing the hills, to have acres that never fail, to have an air washed by mountain clouds and sweet with clover, this is health. This is the natural habitat of the patriot, the author, the philosopher, the artist, and the saint.

It was amidst such an environment that the Greeks turned over all questions that are capable of being handled by the human mind, and suffused their philosophy with an imagery of beauty. They thought out their architecture in view of the mountains. They planned their poems as they looked on the heights.

THE JACKSON REGION

GOING north from Conway we reach the intimate hills at Jackson, and from them we obtain new visions of the loftier peaks. One may say that between Jackson and a point a mile north of the Glen House there are more mountain vistas, perhaps, than elsewhere in the east of the state, and perhaps more than on any other similar stretch of road. The Presidential Range is beautiful in the morning for a considerable number of miles. From points in Jackson itself one gets fine visions of Carter's Dome and Wild Cat. Doublehead appears from numerous standpoints all the way from Conway north and far beyond. Tin, Iron, Black, Moat, and many other peaks, outside of the Presidential Range, have their fine setting in the mountain meadows.

From Jackson village there are several roads running sharply up to the hills on the east, leading to numerous fair hill farms or summer vantage points which have been chosen to recreate the vacationer. From

A WOODBINE DECORATION — TUFTONBORO

A RANDOLPH ORCHARD

MOUNT WASHINGTON BROOK

A CARROLL DRIVE

these hills Giant's Stair appears, and more than one such aspect shows itself under different names.

The birches on these highways are very fine. The streams in the time of full water toss many a foaming and noisy cascade to the valley, where in limpid, restful reaches the mountains are outlined.

While the large resorts are mostly in the valley, and therefore shut off from the more extensive views, their guests maintain that they are stimulated to take long walks to the view-points. Smaller hostelries, boarding-houses, and the like, climb up the sides and crown the crests of the habitable hills, and of course claim as their advantage that they are in immediate view of the best of the White Mountains. Happily, there is enough country, of whatever contour, to please all.

Jackson undoubtedly stands high among the more desirable mountain towns as a goal of visitation. It seems to hold its own very well. It vies in this respect with Bethlehem, Dixville, and the Woodstocks. It differs from the Conways in that it is closely shut in and lacks broad meadows. One is always touching the hills and often climbing them, although the thoroughfare is not a mountain grade.

We had an amusing experience at Jackson, as we had not visited it for twenty years. We dropped down into a well-appointed hotel where we found ourselves to be the only Gentiles! We were very courteously received. Still, whatever the management may have thought, we could not sound the guests, or at least did not think it wise. We therefore removed to another hostelry where all were Gentiles. This is a curious development of summer life which probably will not continue more than another generation as Americans become more thoroughly amalgamated.

On top of these Jackson hills we found a couple of interesting scenes which later we learned were close to the premises of a friend of thirty years' standing, who, indeed, had taught us, in that long ago, which end up to set the camera. It was a mutual delight, and none the less so to us because we had found these themes which he had not yet observed, since

[*Text continued on page* 49.]

THE HILLS OF CARROLL

Hills of Carroll, sweeping wide,
By the old White Mountain-side,

In your glory, do you guess
Half the beauty you possess?

Beauty that is almost pain,
Glimpsed through borders of a lane!

Blossoms in a fragrant mass
Point to some dim mountain pass;

Green of grass and pink of trees
Call the yellow-coated bees;

Soft depths of a wooded crest
Catch the sunrays of the west;

Purples, drifting to the heights,
Fade at last to snowy whites.

And through centuries of time,
Awe-inspiring, grand, sublime,

There the ancient mountains sit,
Worshiping the Infinite!

Hills of Carroll, hills afar,
How near heaven's door you are!

MILDRED HOBBS

CARROLL ORCHARD HEIGHTS

RANDOLPH-GORHAM ROAD

THE FLUME—AMMONOOSAC

PROFILE LAKE PATH

he was not engaged in the necessity of the search. We had a good day together capering over the hills like kids rather than "old he ones." In fact, the hills compel us to be young if one only climbs them. Going down is not so easy. It is a pity that more people do not find this out, for it is positively true that climbing a steep hill is far easier than going down, and far less likely to incur a fall. What a delight it was to find that the sons and daughters of this old friend had grown up to take influential and honorable places in our modern life! They did this the better as they came back annually to draw fresh life and inspiration from these splendid uplands.

THE DIXVILLE REGION

A S WE are now on the east-side road we may as well go the length of the state and take in the most northerly point of general resort, Dixville Notch. The way thither lies partly along the banks of the Androscoggin, which steals away out of New Hampshire and imparts the wealth of its increasing waters to Maine.

Gorham is a good center for mountain and lake excursions. It lies at the junction of the road which, making west, passes north of the main mass of the White Mountains. We go through thriving manufacturing villages, as Berlin, which find their material in their forests.

Dixville Notch has its gemmed lake, Gloriette, made more attractive doubtless by the great care given to its environs. Here is a very large center of summer guests, whose golf course is on the lofty heights, and whose players are said to be well acquainted with the moon, as well as the sun. The man whose imagination created this development did so largely as a matter of love, as all truly great projects are created.

We ventured to the extreme north of the state and the sources of the Connecticut, but the region is comparatively uninteresting and flattens toward the great Canadian plains at the height of land. It is often the

DANIEL WEBSTER BIRTHPLACE

case that on highest lands there are great tracts of water-saturated acres that form valuable sources of power.

If we pass to the south on the west side of the state, through Colebrook, we encounter a great many fine farm lands, and observe a satisfactory number of recurring river-stretches sweeping along the foot hills.

THE JEFFERSON REGION

IT IS perhaps improper to name this district after any one town, since Randolph, Jefferson, Lancaster, Whitefield share with one another in elevation, outlook, fine orchards, birches, forest reaches, and a great degree of natural beauty. Perhaps Jefferson, being somewhat central to

MELVIN PASTURES

BIRCH RIVER—PINKHAM

MOUNT WASHINGTON ROAD

THE OLD MAN PROFILE

the district, may be the better known, and it is certainly the resort of many votaries. We consider that the drive from Gorham to Lancaster may match in its merits any other in the state. Passing just north of the Presidential Range, of which wonderful aspects continually appear, it is south of the Randolph range and of Waumbek, Star King, and other well-beloved masses of bold grandeur. These northern mountains are the last great guardians of the Appalachian chain, as we hardly consider the Maine mountains sufficiently related to be reckoned with in this connection. We passed over this road many times in the apple-blossom season of 1922, and certainly we never reveled more joyously in the delightful contrast between the billowy blooms of the richly-laden orchards and the pale-purple peaks of the ranges against which they were set.

The exigencies of life prevent many persons from seeing the country at its best, which, of course, is in the early spring and the late autumn, but if we had only two weeks in the year to wander in the country we should certainly take them in May, and if that were impossible, in the second half of October.

The summer visitor sees the dense greens and the subdued coloring which seems to have settled down to meet and endure the torrid season, after the exuberance of spring has faded and before the victory of autumn flaunts its multi-colored flag across the broad horizon. Nevertheless, we have tried to bring back to the town dweller the records of these seasons, and to make this volume particularly rich in the spring aspects of northern New Hampshire.

There are those who cannot be weaned from their early love for the Jefferson and Randolph region. Again, there are those who, from the slopes of Lancaster, look south, and have enjoyed for a generation their vantage ground and their fine immediate environment. The villages of Lancaster, Whitefield, Littleton, Bethlehem, and Lisbon, all appear to be of about the same size, though doubtless their residents know this to be otherwise. Each has its peculiar attractions. Littleton is the wideawake, business district of the year around, and Whitefield and Lancaster are centers of a permanent population, whose good lands extend afar and give an odd impression, since one immediately finds oneself on broad plains from a recent experience of the shut-in roads to the east. We like these villages, and ever delight in that sort of residence, which, like that of Conway, can find adequate materials of town development within reach of the presiding and stimulating mountain ridges.

THE BRETTON WOODS REGION

THE approach to Bretton Woods through Crawford's Notch is perhaps the most charming of the several avenues. Most of the way through Bartlett, Bemis, Crawford's, and so on to the summit of the pass we follow the infant Saco,

> *" Rejoicing as it laughs and leaps*
> *Down the gray mountain's rugged side."*

As one looks back, fine glimpses of Mount Tremont appear. Looking forward, the shoulders of the Presidential Range close in upon one so as always to afford some new aspect to occupy us. There are fine sections of wood where one passes through the dense shadows and suddenly emerges upon a bold view. This portion of the mountains is one of the first to be sought, some of the resorts dating back four generations. In fact, as this trail was the first in the region, from the direction of Boston, it became thoroughly well known, and is today perhaps more familiar than any other part of the mountains. Last year, a little below the summit on the right, there was a delicate ribbon of water broken by many rocks, and falling from a great height.

On reaching the crest of the road, one comes at once upon the comparatively level basin with its small pools artificially enhanced by dams, on either side of which lie the celebrated resorts found at Bretton Woods.

THE MEETING OF THE WAYS—ALSTEAD

DOWN THROUGH CRAWFORD'S

MOUNT LAFAYETTE

TWIN MOUNTAIN BIRCHES

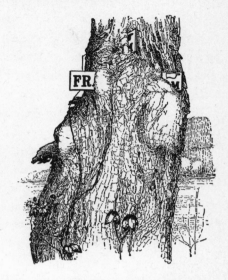

DOOR AT PORTSMOUTH   A SIGN AT HILLSBORO

There are entrancing old wood-roads leading toward Mount Washington from this point. We ventured over some of them by motor without disaster. They are not steep, but here and there in the wet season incline to be bothersome. Being practically disused and carpeted with leaves, they supply just that strength of consolation needed by souls like-minded with Bryant. If it is possible at once to soothe and stimulate the mind, these wood-paths accomplish that contradictory result.

The miniature cascades of the young Ammonoosuc, up which one may walk from Bretton Woods for a very long distance, are always delightful, and afford an abundant number of excellent compositions which have become rather trite in their lower portions, it is true.

The general view of Mount Washington obtained from the valley at Bretton Woods, while quite different from that at the Glen and northwards, is not by many thought any better. Perhaps the finest general aspect of the White Mountains is to be seen at North Conway or Intervale. The most intimate view of the Presidential Range in general is, perhaps, from Pinkham Notch north of the Glen. Other general views of the Presidential Range in Randolph are quite different and to many preferable. The summit of Mount Washington reached by the Glen road is an exhilarating drive. The other method of approach by cog-railroad from Bretton Woods is well known.

We have been fortunate in securing a good number of clear, well-detailed, and cloud-decorated aspects of the Presidential Range from various points at Glen and Pinkham Notch.

The drive from Bretton Woods to Bethlehem or to Profile Notch is more or less tame. Nothing is farther from the truth than that any point in the mountains is attractive. The extensive flats which usually occur in mountainous regions are often quite uninteresting. One needs to seek out the points of special beauty.

Mount Washington, being the loftiest crest in the northeasten part of our country, is appropriately rendered accessible by two routes mentioned, but for the most part, except to those who love to follow the mountain trails, the aspects of this and the other peaks are far more pleasing as viewed from below.

THE BETHLEHEM AND TWIN MOUNTAIN REGION

AT A great elevation above the sea, and with a broad outlook, the Bethlehem region has become the most notable center for tourists in the White Mountains. It is essentially the heart and spirit of summer life. The drives near it are bordered in some cases by exquisite birches, and in other instances open fine vistas of the various peaks. Bethlehem being approachable through Profile and Franconia Notches, as well as through Crawford's Notch and from the north, becomes a natural central point for many mountain excursions.

The drive north from Bethlehem is in many respects among the most

THE LAKE END—ANDOVER

NEW HAMPSHIRE ROAD—NEAR WOLFEBORO

A STODDARD BYWAY

WESTMORELAND WATERS

interesting, and takes one past fine outlooks and resorts at Lancaster to Whitefield, whence one may go on to Dixville Notch.

Bethlehem is, of course, much sought by those who would escape the miseries of hay fever. We cannot, in summer, escape heat, except maybe on the summit of Mount Washington. All other points in the East are at elevations too slight to change greatly the summer temperatures. We have often known the thermometer to stand at the same point in Boston and New York as in the White Mountains, and even oftener have known it to be but slightly less in the mountains than at the great centers of our population. The general impression to the contrary is possibly natural. We mention this curious fact because the idea of going away in the summer to keep cool is based upon insufficient data. It is true, however, that the nights are very much more likely to be cool in the northern part of New England than in the southern. The cogent reason for seeking the mountains in summer is for the purity of the air, the inspiration of the splendid outlines, the glory of the clouds, the scent of the pine trees, and the touch of Nature in her healing and tonic beneficence.

THE PROFILE REGION

WE HAVE at various times called attention to the inveterate and apparently ineradicable habit of the vast majority of people whereby they delight in finding human and animal forms in inanimate nature. The striking profile of the Old Man of the Mountains is perhaps the supreme instance of the public interest in such things. There is no doubt that this odd rock-formation has been more admired than the wonderful lake at its foot, or than the endless and splendid variations of the clouds above it. A very similar profile at the falls of the same name in the town of Hill causes many also to turn aside as at a wondrous thing.

[*Text continued on page 65.*]

FRANCONIA

Franconia sleeps among her hills
And dreams long summer dreams;
A Sabbath stillness rests upon
Her fields and wooded streams.

Her quiet coves and water-nooks
Are brushed with heaven's tints,
And painted with the flying birds
And trees and sunset glints.

Her lily-cups of white and gold
Breathe out an incense-prayer,
And lacy wings of insect-things
Are floating on the air.

And from her dark, sweet evergreens,
Clear in the dreaming hush,
There breaks a lilting ecstasy
Of song; thrush calls to thrush!

The low winds from the sun-kissed hills
Steal silently along
To whisper through the mountain notch
Their peaceful even-song.

So sleeps Franconia below
Her billowing walls agleam;
And in the glow of sunset's peace,
With her my heart would dream.

FOREST POOL—FRANCONIA

A LITTLE LAKE NEAR WASHINGTON

AT PORTSMOUTH

AN ALSTEAD STREAM

Mr. Winthrop Packard, in his "Tales of the Trails," has wittily called attention to a great boulder which has in part a George Washington face and in another a Booker Washington face. It becomes very boresome to be interrupted in the enjoyment of an exquisite outline by some one who detects a lion, a horse, or the features of some president in the foliage or the rocks. We often wonder why these fertile imaginations cannot give poor old Socrates and the old-world worthies a chance. These resemblances are inevitably found to be some notable American political character. This is very remarkable, if true.

After all, it is still the trivial that excites the greatest interest. Perhaps the mountains themselves may in time assist in curing the tendency to see the little and be blind to the great.

We have always had a vast love for the ocean because the waves do not long enough retain their shapes to be named after patriots and sages. Shrewd showmen have always made much of that cheap side of human nature which will pay to see the two-headed calf and any such monstrosity. Beauty is ever at a discount, but it will come to its own at length. Is not education itself, in the large sense, a training to see what is really worth seeing, and to live with those who are worthy of association?

The very great beauty of the Profile Notch, with its two or three little lakes, with its solemn and sheer peaks, with its finely-wooded roads, is a sufficient distinction. The endless cloud-play, as it is influenced by the interference of the summits, is to us the most fascinating aspect of the Profile region.

The burning of the great hotel located at the Notch may pave the way for an erection of a permanent character. The building of summer resorts of inflammable materials was at one time merely an oversight. It has now become a crime.

A home in the mountains ought to blend in its aspect with its surroundings and be of a character suggesting sturdiness, permanence and the beauty of its environment.

THE WOODSTOCK REGION

THE only rivals in broad, general views of the mountains are Woodstock and Conway.   The Franconia Range, considered as an aspect of beauty alone, takes a very high place.   Furthermore, the Woodstocks with their river and their various drives, as that to Lonesome Lake and others, are an admirable rest region, since they are within the capacity of persons of moderate means.

In fact, there are various unheralded resorts in the White Hills known only to those whose good fortune has found out their merits.   Hundreds, probably thousands, of boarding houses or small hotels, conducted by hospitable and excellent people and furnishing adequate though simple provision for human need, are scattered all through these fair valleys.

It is easy to see in the large farm houses the effect of summer visitants for generation after generation.   A wing has been added here and there, and that which was once merely a farm has taken on the aspect of a magnified country place, dear to the hearts of those who have there found their sweethearts, or find bracing air in such environment for their children.   The simple friendships fostered in the hills are among our dearest recollections.

THE WINNEPESAUKEE REGION

THIS great lake, forming one of the most remarkable features of New England geography, cannot at the dictate of fashion be thrust aside from its preëminence in beauty.   The Indians very justly gave it its name, which signifies " the smile of the Great Spirit."   In fact, every great natural feature, especially water features of the world, seems to exist to reflect the grandeur above it.   It is not to the credit of our civilization that the Indians felt this truth more justly than we do.   If we should give to a lake an English name of like significance we should

ANTRIM BIRCHES

A DIMPLED ELBOW—TUFTONBORO

COPLEY'S MRS. MACPHAEDRIS

THE WARNER PARLOR—PORTSMOUTH

A HAMPTON HOME

become butts of ridicule and be thought very queer. The simplicity and directness of the Indian character in this respect merits our attention. Almost all their names were given, as names should be, to designate the salient features of an object. It is true that the poverty of the Indian vocabulary leads them to repeat endlessly, so that we have a Pawtucket, a Pawtuxet, a Shetucket, a Nantucket, and various other forms. But we cannot escape the charge of repetition. How many Echo Lakes are there in New Hampshire? Even in this volume we have been obliged to recognize more than one. It would seem that not only should a human being have some more distinctive appellation than John, but also a body of water and a town should each be favored with a name peculiar to itself.

In some old-world lands it is still the custom to name a child in honor of the saint whose day coincides with its own. Thus poor little children are weighted down with appellations which have no reference to their characters, and are of little use in distinguishing them from others.

Our English ancestors were grievous offenders by the sameness of the names which they gave to places, and even in the same county we find place-names repeated. We in America have been subject to the same lazy process, and have by transferring the name of some notable English town to American acres rendered ourselves commonplace and sometimes ridiculous. In Maine, for instance, the rockiest town known is called Rome. The very name White Mountains is no more distinctive than the absence of a name. Amongst these White Mountains we recall one called Black Mountain. We suppose all mountains are black in some seasons of the year if they are below the snow-line, and all mountains are white in winter, and all are blue in some aspects, and all are smoky, and all are gray, and all are green. At least, about this sameness we can have a good-natured laugh, and in the next world we discover we may apply a more happy system of nomenclature.

Meantime we are sailing on the Winnepesaukee with its sixty odd islands and its aspects of beauty innumerable. Here and there are those who, assured in their own good taste, have their summer residences where they may see the play of light and wind on the broad bosom of the great lake, poured as it is into the hollows of the hills.

The Weirs, given up to the tripper, and similar though smaller resorts, cannot by the crowding of their dwellings overcome the serenity of water, cloud, and upland. The remote southern points of the lake are very wonderful with their bluffs and bold inlets. The city of Laconia, a clean, alert, attractive town at the southeast of the lake and touching directly on Squam, is desirable headquarters for its region. To the north, about Meredith and Center Harbor, one finds drives that mingle agreeably the new outlines of bay, the new curves of wooded-roads, new contours of tumbling hills.

THE LAST LOAD — TUFTONBORO

A WOLFEBORO LANE

A RANDOLPH BROOK

UNDER GREAT PINES — STRAFFORD COUNTY

The islands form, for many, ideal summer homes, as an island in a considerable body of water cannot escape a beautiful view from every quarter. In fact, a mountain country is never so well seen as from an island, and the seclusion and cosiness of island life is combined with the really rapid and adequate communication which modern motor boats provide.

We are very fond of Winnepesaukee, its surface, its shore, its gemmed isles, and the many excellent characters who dwell on its margin the year around. Tastes may change and the tide of fashion may ebb and flow, but Winnepesaukee will always be the supreme instance, on a large scale, of beauty as seen on lake and mountain, each supplementing and doubling the other's attractions.

Of late a gentleman who could feel the call of these sentiments has developed a great mountain resort on the eastern side of the lake. Whether it will eventuate in calling people back to admire and to live with the attractions visible in this district, we do not know, but we are happy in seeing here and there the evidence that we still have men who do things moved by the sense of beauty and romance.

THE SUNAPEE REGION

THE Sunapee region, approached from Concord through Hopkinton and Warner on the east, or from Claremont on the west, opens with much beauty on the sudden view that we get of it at Newbury. It is a lake of many charms, and lying as it does amid lofty hills, and not being very extensive in any part, it affords more pleasing compositions than a larger body of water. This lake has been sought by persons of somewhat quiet tastes, and the character of the summer residents is of that class which loves the natural world and is content with it, at least for the summer season. The circuit of the lake on land or by motor-boat is most agreeable. Each method has its merits. There are lofty bluffs in the drive which give glorious outlooks.

Mount Kearsarge is the great peak of the region, though Mount Sunapee looms immediately over the lake and, therefore, is much more impressive. Mount Kearsarge, by the way, has many faithful admirers, and as one sees it from various lakes or streams it is dreamy and impressive and lovable. We are not among those who are particularly impressed by the awesomeness of mountains, at least in summer. They seem very dear and intimate to us. We love to lie in their little nooks and never feel the oppression of their magnitude. On the contrary, their vast mass is an up-bearing and comforting sensation. They seem to give safety as well as dignity and character to the region which they dominate. We can easily understand the worshipful feeling of the Japanese for their great peak which appears in so much of their art expression.

Newport is the natural center for this region, being an active and attractive town with a street of great width, and with comfortable quarters for those who wish to rest here.

The road through Warner, Waterbury, and Bradford to Newbury is recommended in connection with a drive about Sunapee as affording great pleasure. Kearsarge is often in view; again the Warner River supplies numerous alluring curves; near Bradford are small lakes beyond which the mountains appear. Bradford itself is a most winning neighborhood.

In circling Sunapee we may pause to climb here and there a neighboring height, from which the lake lies in beauty on two or three sides of us. To us the lake always seems as if filling a valley. That is to say, we think of the depressions beneath it, and are always seeing in imagination its depths. It appears to us with a greater charm when so thought of, because its fullness in covering the ruggedness of the valleys is an attractive appeal.

Passing from Newport to Claremont we reach an active year-around center which forms a gate to the central part of the state from the west. This district also spreads abroad many a fertile field, and combines with

GLORIETTE LAKE—DIXVILLE NOTCH

EARLY VICTORIAN — HANCOCK

OLD ROCKINGHAM CHURCH

A DOVER STREET

many other sections of the state in supplying the great marts with milk. The greater part of New England in its smoother sections is now kept up and saved from negligence by the steady demand for dairy products, which do more to beautify a country than any other one agency, now that the keeping of sheep is so rare.

THE PORTSMOUTH REGION

THIS year has seen the celebration of the three-hundredth anniversary of the settlement of what is, next to Plymouth, perhaps the oldest center in New England. It was in 1623 that the Pilgrims of Plymouth had a station at Dover, and Portsmouth dates from the same period. In fact, in the celebrations of the two cities, carried on at the same time, there seemed an unnecessary rivalry, since there is sufficient legend and history for both. There is not, perhaps, anywhere in this country a more thoroughly interesting water-way than the estuary of the Piscataqua. The singularly beautiful harbor of Portsmouth, and the approach thence to Dover along old banks mellow with civilization so old; the fine slopes of Dover point; the reaches of Great Bay and Exeter River; and the other streams that gather here, are all contributory to a general impression of great weight. It is not strange that this district has become the main gateway for travelers in New England who seek the calm, the inspiration, and the beauty of its summers.

Aside from Portland, it perhaps is not rivaled in this respect, and its inland waters are as pleasing as its harbor.

The monumental structure recently completed between New Hampshire and Maine as a memorial to its war heroes is a very fitting and long-needed bond of union, doing away with the mediaeval toll system, and the memories of the rattle-trap past, connected with the passage of the old bridge. When the great span is lifted for the passage of ships one is reminded somewhat of a similar London bridge, only in this instance the dimensions of the river are much greater. This achievement is a notable and striking monument for all time.

Portsmouth itself has appealed to us as the most pleasing of all small shore cities. Its numerous quaint little houses; its scarcely less numerous pretentious mansions, all of the older time; its early churches; its delightsome wharf drives, winding in and out, narrow, tortuous, and old-world-like; its inner basins, as that to the south of Pleasant Street and that on Christian Shore; its quaint public collections, appeal to us so that the cumulative effect of their impression is very great. The center, as it is, of all the beach life from Ogunquit, Maine, to Salisbury, it is one of the most wide-awake small towns imaginable. To those who love at once the old and picturesque, together with some signs that Americans are not dead, Portsmouth appeals strongly.

The navy yard on the Maine side supplies a continuous and unusual

THE MOUNTAINS FROM PINKHAM

THE HEIGHT OF THE SEASON — JEFFERSON

ISSUING THE INVITATIONS

INVESTIGATING AN HEIRLOOM — PORTSMOUTH

note of interest in America, because navy yards are few and far between.

The old houses comprise many of the big three-storied arks of the period about 1800, with important porches, of which type the Pierce Mansion is an example. It is not alone in its dignity. Even as we wander out towards Dover there are large and finely remote dwellings of similar character. We have somewhat largely illustrated the doorways and dwellings of Portsmouth, partly because at one time we rescued the Wentworth-Gardner house in that city from degradation, and therefore spent very much time in the city, and partly because of the inherent attractiveness of the place.

Of course, it is a mark of a still somnolent public sentiment that such a place as the Wentworth-Gardner house was not made a state or city monument, but years ago, when the author was engaged in small necessary restorations of that dwelling, public sentiment had not awakened as it has somewhat since. If the city of Portsmouth should permit this dwelling to be carried away, it would sin against its own light.

The Warner mansion, more than one illustration of which we give, is thought by most to be the first, as it is perhaps the finest, of early examples of the gambrel roof. Its treasures have long remained in one family. Another dwelling near it was recently marked for destruction although it possessed some beautiful and important features.

The preservation of the Ladd house in the hands of one of our patriotic societies is a matter of congratulation. It has many treasures, and its garden is delightful. It would be a long and boresome record should we mention half of the dwellings known in Portsmouth for their fine doors, halls, or rooms. The names of May, Richter, Wendell, Wentworth may serve to summon up to those of us who have made this delightful round many a memory of quaint and quiet beauty.

The drives from Portsmouth along the shores of Little Harbor or about Newcastle are the most obvious near interesting attractions.

Running to Rye and the Hamptons one encounters the bold and rocky shores of the former and the long smooth sweeps of the latter, each appealing strongly to its own kind. We recommend to those who are strangers in this district that they follow some of the back roads of Rye and Hampton, as these roads have many a quaint dwelling and many a sheltered pine nook.

Portsmouth is, of course, the point of departure for the deservedly famous summer colonies of the adjacent corner in Maine. To many, York is the only summer place in the world, but of this further in our Maine volume.

The trip to Dover from Portsmouth, returning by the north shore of the Piscataqua affords fine inland waterway views. The drive to Exeter through Greenland, past the oldest brick house in the North if not in the whole country, where the tenth generation of the same family are now dwelling, is another route of pleasure already alluded to. Of course, the main shore route from Portsmouth south is the best known, but perhaps owing to its trunk character it is least attractive.

We always think of Dover, Rye, Hampton, and York, and the immediately surrounding towns as a resort unit with Portsmouth. They are almost equally early in settlement, and they each appeal with their peculiar attractions.

Portsmouth, to dwellers in eastern New England, is the gateway of New Hampshire both in regards its lakes and mountains, and is also on the only good route into Maine.

It may be as well that Portsmouth is no larger. Nevertheless, we have often wondered why, with its strategic location, it has not developed into a more populous center.

PICTURES OF NEW HAMPSHIRE

WHILE New Hampshire has brought to most of us and to our fathers the chief aesthetic and romantic appeal of the North Atlantic states, it has singularly lacked any general illustration. We have sought in vain for any pictorially adequate representation, and it is,

GLORIETTE NOOK—DIXVILLE

therefore, with special pleasure that we have secured these pictures, with what success we leave the gentle reader to judge.

On page 11 we have illustrated a phase of the Ammonoosuc that has been markedly appreciated. It is on the way to Mount Washington from Bethlehem. In our thought, the combination of a mountain and the stream which flows from it supplies a richness which is fascinating. Afar is a great mountain vastness, and here is the wealth which comes from it.

The Turn Homeward (p. 12) is the entrance to a private estate, satisfactory in its seclusion and the barrier which it presents to the noise and dust of the highway, and The Dell Road opposite is one of those smooth, narrow-winding, wooded ways so dear to the heart of the wanderer.

In Birch Hill Top (p. 15) we have one of several scenes made on or near this spot, showing the Connecticut River through the branches of a most magnificent cluster of birches, perhaps the most beautiful we have ever found, the vast trunks of the fallen trees lying before us, and beyond are their successors still continuing in beauty side by side. This exquisite scene, approved by many, is fully visible from the highway, but up to the time of our visit no one had ever seemed to consider it worth recording. This is one of the amazing things. The moralist would undoubtedly tell us that we go by the best and move on to a point whose location will do us no good unless we are more appreciative than we are now.

Cherry Mountain from an Orchard (p. 20) gives us a very delightful but seldom-sought combination, — the crest beyond the bloom. New Hampshire is wonderful in spring with a great number of such beauties.

Very early in the morning we found Nesting Time (p. 23). Lancaster, indeed, is one of the most attractive towns in the state. Here is the complete pink-and-white glory on the left, and a fine elm on the right, and the path that leads between, a satisfactory filling vision.

Again on the Lancaster-Randolph road we look through the orchards, at the bottom of the same page, and take in the Presidential Range.

We are happy in The Mount Washington Trail (p. 27) in combining blossom, shadow, and the summit of the king among New England peaks.

Carroll also presents in the spring many glorious examples through the orchards. We have often found that by rising with the sun there is found a quiet and serene and almost religious beauty in landscapes. In the White Mountains (p. 31) we were on the spot before the sun topped the crest to our left, and waited until its first gleam shot across the highway. There was perfect silence, the morning coolness, and glisten of the dew, and the promise of a long and wonderful day, which was amply fulfilled. On the same occasion we obtained the other picture on the same page, which is the entrance to a dwelling.

The pictures at the bottom of page thirty-five and at the top of page thirty-nine we found on the same occasion. It was a white day in every sense. We have never seen a tree so effulgently white with apple blossoms as that in the distance in The Mountain Orchard.

The stream flowing through Randolph, along which the road winds thence to Gorham, has here and there very decorative birches intervening between us and the fine crests of the Presidential Range.

It was twenty-five years ago, when first our unwonted eye sought to compose the beauties of New Hampshire, that we found the Sheep in Melvin Pasture (p. 51). They have evidently found a bit of salt by the side of the old log. We will not say that we did not coax them to the spot.

The Meeting of the Ways (p. 55) could also be called The Parting of the Ways. It all depends upon the point of view. Shall we say that all things sometimes diverge and all things some time come together?

How many times at such junctures we have wondered which way to turn, and how many times doubtless we have turned to the wrong road. As a rule, one always suspects that the forsaken way was the better. The effect of choice, however, is something acquired with time and something that may be exercised rapidly. We know of no better training in decisiveness than to make a journey among the hill-roads. We hear much

PORTSMOUTH FROM THE HARBOR

MERRIMAC BANKS

TO RECEIVE US—HANCOCK

A FRIENDLY CROOK—NEWINGTON

of people who are set in their ways. We hear nothing of persons who seem to have no sense of direction or decision what they shall do. If fifty times a day every day in a week they were obliged to decide it might assist their weakness.

About the Twin Mountain House there are many walks that have allured a generation of people. Directly opposite it, looking down through a cluster of birches, the wandering river laves the steep banks. There is almost always a breeze under the trees and here is one of the quiet nooks of the state where seats are comfortably provided, and where one who loves to feel the natural world about him may while away many an hour of desultory reading.

Wandering off into a by-road, in fact perhaps a private road, in Andover, we find at the southern lake end several perfect combinations of birch and shore and path (p. 59).

Westmoreland is one of the beautiful towns of New Hampshire, and the east town of the same name has lovely meadows (p. 60). The road not usually traveled, north and south, near the river, is also beautifully wooded and attractive. Westmoreland village lies off the main track, and is a cosey and desirable nook on that account.

Back of the Forest Hills House is a pool or lake, terms as to which we seem to have no strict definition. The reflections and contours are most beautiful. This part of Franconia is thoroughly pleasing, and its outlooks are quite different, on the Franconia region, from those seen only a mile or so away.

Alstead, while not mountainous, has a great many of those sharp hills which often supply more interest, especially in the way of drives or residence sites than the strictly mountainous districts. Alstead Stream (p. 64) presents many a composition. The route from Bellows Falls through Alstead to the junction of the Keene-Lebanon road is a pleasing piece of forest drive to be highly recommended.

The Antrim Birches (p. 64, 84, 159, 175, 187, 208) are one of the

[Text continued on page 93.]

FALLS OF THE FLUME

"Deep calleth unto deep at the noise of thy waterfalls."

Bursting to foam, the rushing waters sweep
In swift abandon down the rocky flume,
And curl in feathers of a great white plume,
Quivering, swaying as the cascades leap
The rough-hewn terraces. Down past the steep
High walls encompassing a narrow room
Resounding with a humming, drumming boom
Of waterfalls, " deep calleth unto deep."

Where low the droning cavern's hollow bass
Pounds with a rending rhythmic melody;
Where high the cataract to heaven calls
Through shimmering, plashing spray that veils its face;
The old flume echoes hymns of majesty
Sung by the silver tongues of waterfalls.

MILDRED HOBBS

A GIFT OF THE CLOUDS—THE FLUME

THE COVE OF THE BROOK—EXETER-CONCORD ROAD

THE RANGE FROM THE AMMONOOSAC

sigl..s of the state. Dwellers in lower New England have never seen anything of the kind. The bark is of pale salmon color. Some of these trees L.' fair in time to be among the wonders of the world, in an arboreal sense, if they are carefully preserved. Many of these great trees have not yet reached their growth, and in this climate they reach splendid proportions. The best of them, through neglect, recently fell. Being the largest known, it merited a little care. Still, do what we will with an old tree, we cannot as a rule retain it more than a few years. Birches, especially, are short-lived trees, not rivaling the elm in this respect, and still less the oak and chestnut.

A great many years since we enjoyed immensely several summer weeks on the quiet western banks of Winnepesaukee. In The Last Load (p. 71), we found the ancient, conventional, two-wheeled ox-cart still in use. This vehicle has never had any rival in its capacity to get about on rough ground. The patient oxen, never nervous, put their great strength against the yoke, and take the vehicle steadily over protruding ledges and around the sharpest corners without danger or difficulty. It will be a sad day when this vehicle entirely disappears. Every year probably sees a great many two-wheeled carts abandoned. The boy raking after, the checked shirts of the pitchers, the old stone-wall beyond, the out-cropping ledges, all bespeak the work of our early fathers in a graphic manner.

We have noted that in the town of Sutton there are said to be five hundred miles of stone-wall. This fact is given as a reason for the hardness of life in such towns. It ought rather to be given as a reason for dwelling in such towns. If stone-walls are made and the great body of rocks removed from the fields, then, the pioneers, work having been done, the sons ought certainly to thrive where their sires with a greater handicap throve. The bare fact is that the fathers built the stone-walls and lived well, and the sons with no walls to build seem to live meagerly.

There is no just reason for putting the burden for failure on the country. Its soil is strong and far more free from obstruction than that found in Florida, far less liable to drought than the western prairies, far more convenient to market than regions supposedly more favorable. Nor is it true that dwellers in these towns are altogether unable to thrive. Suppose a farm has a hundred such acres as those before us. At least half of them can be better cared for and the balance be left to pasture. It is a happy circumstance that the market for hay is decreasing, because the tendency will be to consume it on the farms and increase the amount of live stock.

An important underlying and generally unnoticed tendency is the abhorrence by the thoughtless city man and the thoughtless country dweller, and his wife, of anything old. If the dwelling is old it is not repaired but abandoned for a new one not nearly so good. It is a very frequent thing to see two dwelling houses on a farm. One of these has been abandoned as a dwelling and is used for storage. Its beautiful wood-work, consisting of panels, quaint stairs, good fire-places, and hardware in excellent taste, are passed over with contempt. A new dwelling, having no merits whatever except newness, is sought instead. All this may be overcome if the present stimulus and taste to conserve the old extends far enough to take hold of the unthinking citizen. Many of these farm houses can be made very beautiful simply by care. We are not theorizing, but speak what we know because we have restored not a few such dwellings, and not only city dwellers but even the farmer neighbors were high in their praise of the result, and would all be satisfied to dwell in such a home.

What is true of the dwelling is also true of the acres. It is amazing how fashion dominates even labor, and especially that most respectable form of labor, agriculture. There are vast areas in New Hampshire perfectly adaptable for orchards that are being allowed to go back to forests. It is not, indeed, the worst thing that they should be allowed to grow noble forest trees. Most Americans, however, are too impatient to wait a hundred years or even fifty years for a crop. We observe with pleasure that New Hampshire farmers are getting together to plan the standardization of their fruit products so as to compete with the far inferior fruit of the West, which has the handicap of a journey across the

JAFFREY WATERS

THROUGH THE BIRCHES—PINKHAM

STREATHAM WATERS

SPRING IN NEW HAMPSHIRE — LANCASTER

continent, and its origin in a warm climate where it lacks the flavor of New England apples.

It is not merely, however, in fruit culture that such acres as these may be made valuable. It is only necessary to see one thrifty farm in such a town to know what every farm might be. The life history of a man who has made good on such a farm, if carefully studied, will be found to be replete with more practical interest than that of many an artist, author, or statesman. It will appear how he has divided his time, and how he has conserved and improved the natural advantages about him. It is in imitation of such a successful farmer rather than the imitation of a genius that the salvation of America is to be found. It will be learned that this successful man has no genius except the desire to be busy, and no wisdom except that of always having a variety of products for sale. He must be of a serene and well-balanced mind. He must have confidence in his climate, his state, and his acres. He must have at least sufficient intelligence to know that where others have succeeded he also may succeed. We are not saying that conditions do not change, nor are we saying that there are no ups and downs in the farmer's life. Does not the merchant also experience some ups and downs? Among the many statements about the farm failures, why does not somebody mention the many business-house failures? Why does not somebody call attention to the fact that on New York's smartest business street many concerns open in a flamboyant way and run along a little while and go to pieces? In the long run the farmer makes good, because even in a bad year he eats.

This year in which we are is one of the severest for farmers, especially in the Northeast where a drought scarcely paralleled in intensity has blasted the hopes of the farmers. Even so, many of them can exist for the winter without borrowing, and as most of them have a little balance to serve as an emergency fund, they will certainly thrive better than he who has a million bushels of wheat that he has bought at a good figure and must sell for less.

[*Text continued on page* 105.]

FLOATING LEAVES

The forest, in her cloak of painted leaves,
Tears off her golden sleeves
 From long arms bare,
To wrestle with the jovial autumn wind;
And the crisp leaves, unpinned,
 Whirl through the air.

Her gorgeous raiment falls! High in the wood
But yesterday it stood,
 One with the tree.
And now upon the river's blue it floats;
Like fleets of gilded boats
 Sent out to sea.

How like the autumn leaves drift you and I,
Not knowing when nor why
 The fitful breeze
Will bear us out upon the tossing air,
Far from the sheltering care
 Of forest trees,

On great adventures of the Vast Unknown,
Over the ocean-blown
 Eternity!
Like them, on Love's deep bosom shall we float,
Each life a tiny boat
 Set out to sea!

MILDRED HOBBS

BIRCH SANCTUARY—MARLOW

A MANCHESTER DRIVE

CATHEDRAL AISLES

I like to wander down the miles
Of all the wooded churchly aisles,
Where high the columns of the pines
Lift up their rugged, solemn lines,

And spread a latticed canopy
Where squirrels race from tree to tree,
As lacy boughs of oak and pine
In friendly beauty intertwine.

I love the long, dark shadows thrown
Across thick carpets, needle-sown,
By sunbeams slanting bright and brave
From the stained windows of the nave.

I love the pewee's gentle notes,
Whose little sermon softly floats
Above a pool where lilies lie
With faces lifted to the sky.

O sweet responses of a thrush,
That break upon the twilight hush!
O benedicite! where dim,
Far woods send up their hermit's hymn!

I know, when lamps of colored light
Are twinkling in the dome of night,
That angels swing them high the while
To light this great cathedral aisle.

MILDRED HOBBS

SONGS OF THE ASHUELOT

From the crystal mountain pool
Forever springing,
To the lowlands, lush and cool,
I wander, singing;
And the golden rod and the Joe-Pye-weed
And the blue flag hiding in rush and reed
And the beaded tips of the grassy mead
Press over the banks, and wave
To the foam-feathered Indian brave,
The Ashuelot.

But far in the forest glades
The trees are bending,
And I through the sylvan shades
My course am wending,
To rest and dream with the rainbow trout
In the sheltered deeps; then, purling about,
To leap in the fray with a song and shout,
And a thousand jewels toss
At the glistening stones that cross
The Ashuelot.

With a rush through the rock-barred way,
In a flash of white,
I sing to the dazzling day
And the starlit night.
And down through the years, my hills have smiled
With the joy of the music, sweet and wild,
Of their singing, wandering Indian child,
The Ashuelot.

MILDRED HOBBS

AMERICAN COLORS—GILSUM

THE HOMEWARD TURN—CHARLESTOWN

ON THE CONCORD-PORTSMOUTH ROAD

To return to the stone-walls, since they are worthy of it: they are at once monuments of the past and afford a comfortable sense of the presence of other generations still with us. If, as in many cases, they are no longer needed, they serve admirably for road-making, and good numbers of them have disappeared in this way. We could wish that at least those bordering the highways might remain, as there is nothing else which gives a comparable feeling of security, quaintness, and country charm.

In The Wolfboro Lane (p. 71) the cows are coming home. Daily in the westering light they bring their wealth to the barn door, and the one in the foreground will surely provide a rich, yellow ration which is the life of childhood and the joy of age. The sweet-breathed, soft-eared, sleek-skinned heifer, though without a pick to dig gold or coal, and with no efficiency expert except the sun and rain to help her, returns to the farmer a greater yield than the mines, and she leaves her treasures on our very premises, and not where we must go after them.

The black and white Holsteins and the brindle cows offer fine color contrasts. They are as beautiful as the autumn leaves above them, and if we know their habits it is not difficult to induce them to pose for pictures.

New Hampshire is marked in its southern and central portions by a great many huge pines, which stand in small clusters or in solitary majesty. A pine bough, in its form and color, in the shadow which it affords and the soft sough in which it tells its story, is one of Nature's highest achievements in beauty and in suggestion. The pine has not been thought to be very picturesque, but for ourselves, at least, we prefer it to the birch, and in fact above every other tree except the oak and the elm.

FRIENDLY CROOKS

WE WERE amused by a challenge of the title on page eighty-eight from one who had not heard this term applied to the characteristic elm-branch, which comes out like a crooked elbow to take our arm. This particular instance in New England has a second similar crook branching from the first one. Even this second crook is not so very rare, but the first is one of the greatest charms of the elm. It invites us to hang the swing there, or to make a seat among the sparrows, and to watch the robin listening for worms. This has been a bad year for worms. The hard soil has not encouraged them. The robin, true to his habit, hops along patiently, and listens in vain. He must have lived this year largely on other foods, but he is evidently especially fond of a fine, juicy worm. The youngsters look on awkwardly while father and mother, who have just weaned them, are diligently listening. We suppose the surplus fat of the young robin works off in a few days while he is starved to it.

It may be humiliating, but it is a universal law of which we are continually reminded, that beauty and grace are dependent almost wholly on hunger, not only amongst birds but among human kind. The connection between genius and an empty stomach is intimate and almost continuous. Undoubtedly the capable person, after once that capability is developed, comes to derive a certain joy from accomplishment; but in the beginning of labor, while one is awkward, it is sheer necessity that drives, especially if shame is dead. We must, therefore, climb down from the Friendly Crook and seek out more beauty.

THE GIFT OF THE CLOUDS

MILDRED HOBBS has well expressed the thought of our picture on page ninety-one. We were happy in finding a good body of water last season in The Flume. The lower portion of this deep-cut

MOUNTAIN WATERS

A KEENE ROAD

CHEERY MAY—LANCASTER

AMMONOOSAC BEAUTIES

gorge is not as pleasing as the fine tumble of waters at its beginning. How much the country depends, not only for its life but for its beauty, on the little falls or rapids of the brooks! It is not true, however, that we find as many waters in the hill-country as in a level region. The waters of a meadow remain with us longer and spread wider. In the hills, especially the higher hills, there is a rapid hurrying away of whatever the heavens send down, so that in a few days, even in a few hours, the steeper torrents are pretty well exhausted. We enjoy best one of these brooks which has lived long enough to get nearly down to the plains, yet still turns and hastens over miniature cascades where the ferns cluster at the small nooks, and where the great arms of the ash and the maple reach far over the stream to meet their companions.

A WORLD OF ROCK

A BROOK has a way of reminding us that if we scratch the surface we find the earth to be all stone. To be sure, here and there it is molten, but even when it issues from the mountain in lava it soon reverts to its harder state. No doubt it would appear in a plains country that soil is the constituent of the earth from which, indeed, it derives its other name. But, amidst all the hard sayings about the hard stones of New England, we ought to remember that our great plains cities find it necessary to keep on going down for their foundations for about one hundred feet, until at last, after vast expense and labor, they come in contact with the stone which they affect to despise in New England. It would be the part of wisdom to find a use for these stones rather than to say mean things about them. The world is a poorly-founded world so far as its civilization is concerned. Its edifices are shaky, the English cathedrals being mostly built on mud and the early American city edifices in the Mississippi valley being founded on the same unstable material.

We remember recently seeing a driveway all of native ledge which had required only here and there a little dressing away. The sense of solidity afforded by approaching a dwelling itself also on the same foundation was very satisfactory. We imagine that a great deal of the charm of old castles arises from their suggestion of eternity. There was an era, early in the eighteenth century, when every other novel had a castle in its name. There must be a very fundamental human sense that loves the enduring. Stones have a prominent place in poetry as well as in architecture and art. The Psalms are full of references to great rocks and the strength of the hills, the fortresses and watch towers which remind one of divine continuance and security. Somebody said some time that stones in New England were a bad thing, and at once everybody seemed to admit it. We arise in our humble place to contradict this long entertained but wholly erroneous notion. The stones of any country are its glory, or can be made so.

It is not without significance that Borglum has been engaged to sculpture the face of a southern mountain to show there on a scale unique at least in America the progress of the armies of the Lost Cause. It is a move in the right direction. Instead of imagining some grotesque form of rock to represent some politician who is dead, and is, therefore, a statesman, let us engrave the great deeds or the complete heroisms or the splendid discoveries of our age on the cliffs. We imagine that very few will claim a deeply sentimental interest in generations to come, one or two thousand years hence. It is difficult to love what does not exist, just as Mark Twain found it difficult to weep at the tomb of Adam who presumably was no longer there. Nevertheless, one in time comes to have a great joy in the pleasures of imagination, and it is in imaging forth on the sky of the future a worthy human scheme that many find much delight in those otherwise unfilled hours of wakeful nights.

Aside from stone walls, and, lately, their consumption in rock breakers for roads, the stones of New England have been put to little use. Ignored for building materials, and calling for admiration only when some high-balanced boulder gets the name of Rocking Stone, stone has been little admired. Nevertheless some great edifices of granite and marble

LANCASTER BIRCH CLUSTERS

HILLSBORO WATER

BETHLEHEM BORDERS

VILAS FARM—ALSTEAD

TWO PORTSMOUTH DOORS

have arisen from this inexhaustible wealth, and in process of time we
have no doubt the most lasting and glorious evidences of our civilization
will be the numerous edifices yet to arise from these materials. We are,
however, chiefly interested not in one vast structure but in the adaptation
of the natural wealth of New England for the homes of its people, by
the beautiful small, ledge-washed, flaked stones, or by the larger, irregu-
larly-shaped masses, or by the hewn forms prepared for dwellings.

It is a strange and perhaps ominous fact that in these days when we
touch stones we require a long purse. The masons of old Italy were

natural builders, and we note here and there Italian immigrants have erected stone dwellings with the usual unsatisfactory low-pitched roof, used in semi-tropical regions where it does not snow. When a great body of men of various callings become enthused by the idea of permanent edifices, stone work will grow popular and easy to secure. We look forward to a complete change in American homes within a hundred years. By that time, if we are to endure, we shall cover our country with beautiful structures built of stone and built on stone. This is the cement age, and already an extensive and expensive propaganda, financed by the allied manufacurers of cement, succeeds in inducing the use of this material. If we cannot have the native rock, of course cement is the next best thing, but if willing workers are present the natural stone will be no more expensive and far more picturesque.

We remember living in childhood near a very famous granite quarry where shapes that split a little awry, and therefore were very slightly under dimensions, could be had for drawing away. It is still true that such shapes may be obtained near quarries for a very modest sum. People will do what they wish to do. People will do what is fashionable. We follow trends, and caught in such a trend it is almost impossible to escape it. If only a trend toward permanent structures can be started, the greatest material benefit to America will result.

AUTUMN GLORY

A MERICAN Colors (p. 103) was so named because we were met by the red, white and blue, — the blue of the water and the sky, the red of the forest and the white of the birch trunks. It is one of those admirable pictures opened to us by the new road from Keene to Lebanon. Various other scenes of equal beauty are to be found by branching off from this road and seeking out the streams or lakes in the hills.

Hillsboro has much of merit and particularly to those who love the hills

LAUGHING WATER—GREENFIELD

AN EPPING SHORE

MANCHESTER—EXETER ROAD

in conjunction with farming scenes. Especially in autumn the splendid trees of this town are in their variety and richness scarcely surpassed. There are a number of single- or double-arched stone bridges in this region. They are thought by the people to be unusual and attractive. They were quite rare a few years since, but the march of improvement is happily bringing them in here and there, though the beautiful native, undressed stone is not much used these days.

Hillsboro has its beautiful farms, their fences and roadsides studded with elms and maples, and above are the loftier hills completely wooded so that in their flaming banners of Autumn they lift as it were a celestial flag. It was from these colors and the stars above them that we may presume our national emblem was derived.

At the Vilas Farm (p. 112) we were happy in securing what is so hard to be had, the cattle at their stanchion row. The friendly old pair of oxen are reaching for that luscious green fodder. Is there any finer rural scene than the heads of cattle along the length of the barn floor, canopied by the hay in the scaffold and facing the great mow on the other side?

It was not without reason that Denman Thompson, whose drive is shown (p. 279) in Swanzey, spent his summers at the great, open barn-doors, and looked out upon the rural landscape and looked in upon the softly-breathing cattle. There his chair remains in memory of his most interesting career, and still more particularly in memory of the simple and wholesome tastes of the man.

When, as in boyhood, space under another scaffold was left for the cattle, first the oxen, then the steers, then the milch cows and sheep, and the pair of horses looked out from the head of the row of the yearlings down to the calves just large enough to tie up, we had, together with two or three smaller calves in their pen and the hens clucking about the barn floor, a complete assemblage of rural joys. The first pictures of childhood that appealed to us were those of an English farm-yard. No one seems to be doing American farm-yards.

Sheep and lambs in the winter time, with hay above them and a shed beyond them, were cosily protected from the storm. Nothing gives the sense of warmth in a barn like a well-filled scaffold of hay which is completely impervious to the bitter cold. Here on the barn-floor was the farmer's office. Here he traded, planned, petted his stock, and was sufficiently like Adam to joy in the beasts he had named.

The noises of the farm-yard are as full of music and poetry as any classic could be. The clucking of the hens; the occasional high soprano of a little lamb, with the answering contralto of its mother; the deep low of the older cattle; the growling diapason of the bull; the whinny of the horse; the baying of the dog at the door, as he looks at a vehicle coming down the road, — all go to make up a pastoral concert of a most pleasing and stimulating nature. When the grasshopper also quivers its shrill wings, and the bobolink ripples over the ploughed field, the robins sing, the swallows twitter and chuckle as they come back to their nests in the roof, and every living thing utters its language, we hear the music of nature played in all its variations, never the same yet always with the familiar air carried through. Perhaps it is the experience of a half a million years' contact with domestic animals, and perhaps in part it is the poetic appeal, and in part the sense of plenty and comfort, and in part what would serve as a confidence and acquaintance between the man and his beasts, that go to make up the charm of country life in its more intimate contacts.

How many boys hark back to the day when they loosed the hungry calf and brought it to the anxiously-waiting mother? How its tail quivered with delight at the sweet draught! What a Madonna-like head was turned to watch the greedy baby! And, when we go over to the side where the lambs are, we find them kneeling down to draw their feast from the full udders! Where there are twins it is a picture of domestic delight to see one on each side of the mother getting its rich supper.

Perhaps it is not altogether a misfortune that the farm does not seem very profitable when carried on second hand. In order to derive the

HER FATHER'S HALLS—GARDNER HOUSE, PORTSMOUTH

A GEORGIAN ROOM—GARDNER HOUSE

GOOD NIGHT—GARDNER HOUSE

CANOEING ON SUNAPEE

best from it in financial profit as well as in the human delight in labor, the farmer must do the work himself. When the little boy or girl runs out to reach for his rough hand, and walk up and down with him before the great horns of the beasts, we have the completed cycle of rural life, for the mother has called. It is supper time. With a comfortable weariness we go, young and old, into the great home room, for the hulled corn, or the bannocks, or some other delectable dish that will not fade from memory of childhood despite all the wars and earthquakes.

New Hampshire raised such families. There was Daniel Webster's, whose birthplace now restored and preserved by the state we show (p. 155). With its arched shed and its well-sweep and curb, its little lights of glass and its sturdy chimney, it is a good monument in memory of that master mind, one of whose best features was its touch of humanity. It was this home to which he referred in the famous log-cabin campaign speech: " If ever I am ashamed of it, and if ever I fail in affectionate veneration for him who reared it, may my name and the name of my posterity perish forever from the memory of mankind! "

Neither a log cabin nor any other sort of home can make a great genius, but with other concomitants it may make him over or diffuse through him a spirit of helpfulness to the common life with its needs, its hopes, and its loves. Approached from Franklin, this birthplace is more and more becoming a pilgrimage, not for any special value or quantity of relics that remain in memory of New Hampshire's greatest son, but because it is a stimulating sense of inspiration to know that the best life comes from such homes. There is a vast, aged elm a little beyond the home place. It is easily possible that Webster played beneath it, as the tree is said to have been planted by his father. Webster never ceased to love the country life. He was particularly fond of returning to it between the court sessions or after the adjournment of Congress. Almost all really great men love the country, and the greater they are the more do they love it; the more do they feel that their strength comes from it;

[*Text continued on page* 125.]

MORNING IN THE FOREST

In the cool hush of morning
When the dripping trees and grasses
Are adorned with the opals of the sky,
Through the dim forest clearing
Creeps the flush of sunrise, stealing
To the banks where the sleeping waters lie;

Where the mist on the river
Is a clinging silver blanket,
Spread in folds on the dreaming stream below,
Till the morn's rosy fingers
Catch it softly from the shadows,
And the gray cloud is lifted in the glow.

Swiftly gone, in the silence,
All transparent as a phantom,
Blushing deep with the kisses of the dawn;
Through the tall trees it rises
In a rainbow-tinted vapor,
And is lost from the forest, heaven-drawn.

Then the boughs drip with jewels,
And the waking river sparkles,
And the lane is a poem beyond words!
Ah, the song of the beauty
Of a morning in the forest
Is a song for the singing of the birds!

MILDRED HOBBS

MORNING IN THE FOREST—KINGSTON

GLEN BIRCHES

AN OCTOBER WOODLAND—KINGSTON

the more do they understand the unity and harmony of nature; the more do they derive suggestion, inspiration, and recreation from the scenes of their childhood.

Another such home we have called "Protected" (p. 128). The great, double tree looms with massive bulk over the small roof which has seen several generations pass, through the ebb and flow of its career. It now stands as their monument, and however little it may be conscious, in our sense, yet it knows more of them than any one else. They sleep forgotten, but in their day how patient and willing they were!

Many jokes, some not good-natured, are current in regard to the average man. But that man is, as a rule, when you know him well, possessed of many kindly and reasonable traits. "He gets along," as the pithy phrase of the country has it, with the rest of the human race. He fits in somehow, and helps to make the completeness of the world, and to keep up our confidence in the decency of the species.

COUNTRY MYSTERY

WHAT is beneath the waters in Autumn Mystery (p. 131)? Do not imagine that there is merely a broken reflection there and a touch of wrinkling wind on the surface. We know better than to think that any of us can see all the meaning of a stream and the trees that border it and drink from it and the sky that hovers above it. Its meaning, even in the matter of continuance, transcends us. It is older than we, and will flow when we have changed into some other shape. It has had such experience, it has furnished such life to its swimming denizens, and its gift to the trees and the grasses; it has reflected so much beauty and has heard so many secrets from the branches, that in most ways it seems wiser and more dignified than we humans are. When the brook tells us its whole story, or when we are able to interpret its hints, we shall all be scholars and poets. We shall know the beginning and the end.

It is the mystery in nature whereby the white lily, the blue gentian, the brilliant flame leaf, all spring from the same soil; it is the mystery in the cloud form and in the leaf color; it is the chemistry of vegetation, and that fascinating undefined line between the organic and the inorganic, that give to the meditative their religion.

If we think back far enough, the prospect, could we have viewed the sedimentary or igneous rocks before the teeming life of today, would not have been bright. When first did the breaking down of the rocks afford a field for exploitation by the earthworm? We have been told recently that there is a living creature which can penetrate cement, at least when it is poorly mixed. The scholar feels himself as completely lost as any child when he seeks to imagine the beginning of things, when he seeks to ask whether it was through fire or water that life first became conscious of itself.

The joy of the country is very greatly enhanced because it is a library of history and of prophecy. We grant that it is difficult to read, that few read it at all, that none read it fully, yet all are intrigued by its semi-revelation of a glory and a mystery that we cannot quite reach here. The changing year, the flying snowflake, the leaping trout, the harebell in a spoonful of earth under the shelf of a rock, and a thousand more suggestive, enticing hints are, as it were, the letters of some sublime alphabet which we cannot yet assemble into words, still less into sentences.

If, indeed, we are in this age to come to the religion of nature, we certainly are coming to no mean religion. The modern and we believe quite generally accepted view of the unity of creation forces us to believe that, whatever the religion of nature, it is the same as that of the spirit. Religion is a big and thoroughly-abused word as, indeed, all great things are abused and misunderstood. Considered very broadly and scientifically, perhaps religion is merely the effort to understand and harmonize with the universe. In this sense every chemist worthy of the name may be said to be a religious man, and a superficial person who merely uses old phrases, now meaningless, is not necessarily religious but only talking the jargon.

ELMSIDE — DERRY

RUSSET, WHITE AND GOLD — EXETER

BONNIE BANK — NEWMARKET

PROTECTED — EXETER

We believe that Edison has lately stated that when one cuts a finger and the chemical processes begin to knit the gash, an intelligent power is at work there. Mr. Edison has been quoted often as an unbeliever. But a deep, scientific assurance imbedded in such a statement as that attributed to him is a fine foundation for a religious life.

Doubtless it is possible for one to ramble around the country, treading down its ferns and flowers and careless of its beauties and having merely the instincts of a hunter or a vandal, but we do not believe that this is the common mood of those who wander in the woods or by the streams. Persons who love vegetation do not generally indulge in low appetites or lack a reflective and reverential faculty. The best modern thought, by which we mean the deepest and the most earnest and the most thorough, can but be enthralled by the half-revelations in nature. What we see of the fair world is obviously but a small part of its reality, its power, and its beauty. The latent joys are mostly yet to come to light. The chemical combinations, so unerring in their processes, so marvelous in their results, so mysterious in their action, fascinate us by their mystery at the same time that they raise our respect to the degree of worship. The absolute dependability of chemical forces to do the same things under the same conditions and their inherent might so tremendous as to hold in minute organisms the potentialities of vast results, — all these things partake of what were formerly accounted divine characteristics.

The botanist, the geologist, the astronomer are all dealing all the time with ultimate things. Evolution, so far from being godless and cold, is now perhaps the mightiest of all religious stimulants. It shows a rise in the forces of life and a higher and finer application of power. It is the open and inerrant bible written on the rocks and in the flowers. Affection, which now must be studied in a scientific way, is seen to be at work over the chemical forces. The impulse to friendliness and the apparent appreciation of beauty, would almost seem to exist in the atoms themselves.

[*Text continued on page* 133.]

AUTUMN MYSTERY

When Twilight swiftly dips her brush
And touches earth with mystic tints;
When trees along the river stand
Like phantoms, drawing shrouds of mist
About their garments torn; and bend
As though, but having risen from
The limpid waters of the wood,
They contemplate the shadowy forms
Within the depths from which they came;
And when the river's surface lies
Like velvet in the golden haze;
When the dim sky is softly streaked
With opalescent afterglow;
The air is filled with mystery,
The mystery of autumn days!
The sugar maples' gorgeous leaves
Withering, fading in the dust;
The passing of the gentian's fringe,
And my own hands caressing it;
Are all a part of something strange —
The unreality of things
That seem to throb with life to-day,
And then, to-morrow, seem to die.

But O the mystery of dreams!
The spirit of me laughs with joy
In the sweet Presence of the Real!
It sees abiding beauty through
The shadows of a dying day —
Abiding beauties of a path
The feet are treading, here and now!

MILDRED HOBBS

130

AUTUMN MYSTERY — KINGSTON

THE MILL ROAD — NEWMARKET

A RIVER BOWER — NEWMARKET

At least it is safe to assume that the intelligent person finds the highest charm in those phases of the natural world which keep hinting of greater beauty and more wonderful revelations in store for us, as we delve deeper in the combinations of chemical forces. The very word "chlorophyll" contains in itself an encyclopedia of mystery and the germ of a theology.

Celia Thaxter, in her little book on the Isles of Shoals, calls attention to the pleasing shapes of the infant fishes in comparison with the ugly forms they assume when grown. On the other hand, there are relics of a lower life, such as the remnants of the gills in an unborn child, which indicate that certain ugly forms are being outgrown. We see what has often been counted to be a contest in nature. It is easy to understand why the Persians recognized a god of good and evil. The same notion appears in Christian theology, except that Satan is counted very subordinate and not really divine. All this arises, of course, from the obvious effort in the natural world to handle cantankerous materials in such a manner that they will be harmonious and brought into a finer and higher type of being. Regarded in this sense, it is easy to see why evil is misunderstood by some and counted to be merely inertness.

The persistent growth of weeds without cultivation, and the delicate growth of more useful food plants which must be fostered and protected as against weeds, is another way of reaching natural conditions which reflect the philosophy of good and evil. It is not, therefore, true that nature is ever simple or wholly comprehensible. Forms of great beauty do indeed appear without the touch of man's hand. On the other hand, numerous fruits and flowers are the consequence of careful and age-long development. Thus we see the mystery of forces, more or less external to the fruit and flower, being applied to their care, restraining certain of their tendencies and stimulating certain others. So here is the mystery of a development in nature watched over by man. The interplay of chemical forces, mostly independent of us, as the constant breathing of air, is necessary for our thinking and for our attempts to better the combinations of other forces. So the interplay of the powers in the natural world, between intelligent and unintelligent, is going on in a subtly mysterious manner. It requires an age to take a step in understanding some of these processes. It would almost seem that we would never get very far. We have arrived at the power of using many observed chemical tendencies, but to define those chemical elements accurately, or to see them even with the best instruments we are likely to develop, is perhaps beyond human power as now developed or ever to be developed. We are, therefore, merely on the strand of an ocean too broad to cross, and on that account the more intriguing by its mystery.

Another aspect of mystery is the subtle question, how much our enjoyment of the natural world arises from our own physical alliance with it, or more generally and still more mysteriously our chemical alliance with it. We do, indeed, admire the form of a pine bough, but that admiration does not depend wholly upon the form of the bough. We recognize our affinity with the physical universe. We are brothers not, as Bryant would say, of the insensible rock, but of the rock coming to sensation. This trend of thought carried too far has led to a too close identification of man with nature and God, and has received the name of Pantheism. Nevertheless, in these days every natural student is half way a pantheist. He may not, indeed, recognize personality in the tree as did the Greek legends, but our modern thought has shown us that the elements in the tree and in our own physical natures at least are the same. We may think of a tree as endeavoring to come to consciousness. It certainly responds to the light and to the breezes. It grows to a finer and nobler development if it is within the reach of good soil and congenial air. It weeps when we wound it, and, as in the maple, seems to lack the power to heal its own wounds, whereas the pine can do so.

We may almost say that there is nothing in the natural world which has not some of the marks of consciousness and some of the attributes of personality. The sensitive plant and various flora that seem to be allied to fauna are endlessly fascinating studies of that vague line between what we call consciousness and unconsciousness. When we see a very dull and

EXETER'S LITTLE RIVER

WHEN THE WOODS ARE STILL

A WALLSIDE PATH—TAMWORTH

CHOCORUA FROM THE SACO

evil man and a very glorious, highly-developed blossom, we begin to wonder whether our conventional standards of value are correct. The man seems to have lived in vain or worse than in vain, whereas the flower has spread its glory all about. This mysterious under- or over-development calls the attention of the naturalist. He who can see more in the green leaf and in its autumn change to scarlet than another, by so much more enjoys the glory of out-doors. It is not true, as has often been said, that knowledge brings sorrow. This statement is merely true so far as it goes, but states very much less than half the truth. Investigation and comparison of natural and physical forces is a great and lasting joy.

ANCIENT NEW ENGLAND INSTITUTIONS

THE Town Pound of Durham (p. 157), an ancient construction restored, is a good example of a custom now passed away. When every man was a farmer and every farmer's chief wealth was live stock, a great number of wandering cattle that broke bounds was the inevitable consequence. Some of the old town-pounds are highly interesting for the height and massiveness of their walls, so that no horse, however highstrung, could leap them, and no bull could batter them down. It is pleasing to see here and there such an old custom recorded in the preservation of the pound. We use the phrase in speaking of " impounded water " and in various other ways.

The church spires, usually white, which mark the villages of New England are the outstanding feature of man's work there. The village meeting-house of Hancock (p. 163), seen near or afar, is excellent in line and suggestion. As one goes down over the hills into a village, the spire often appears against the green of an opposing hill, an aspect which adds greatly to its impressiveness.

Southern New Hampshire is studded with many spires of much beauty.

The interior of St. John's Church, Portsmouth, is one of the older examples of ecclesiastical architecture in the state (p. 220).

There are in this volume as seen in the distance, various other spires or lanterns of old churches, serving to accentuate and center the village life. We purposely do not make architectural works of our volumes, but only attempt now and then to show the quaint settings of some of the old public or private edifices.

Town-houses are too often rather bare and unattractive, but here and there, as in the notable recent work of Mr. Cram at Peterboro, we are having a practical application of the truth that beauty is consonant with village life.

The town pump has vanished. If a solitary exception remains in a county it is all we may look for. The village commons, often originating as common pasture or parade grounds, are rather rare in New Hampshire. In Hanover, however, there is an old square largely surrounded by college or ecclesiastical edifices. The old village greens, another name for the commons, are mostly neglected. Of course, the necessity felt in the city for an open plot was not recognized in the country, and, provided the growth of a town was not beyond its original lay-out, no great loss has resulted. Perhaps the most pleasing open spaces in the villages are those which have no regular contour or recognized purpose beyond the fact that they are the natural open centers around which cluster the best old houses.

The library can scarcely be counted an ancient New England institution. It was not until styles in architecture declined that public edifices for libraries were erected. The beautiful library of Nashua (p. 293) is a fine modern expression of what can be done with an irregular piece of ground near the center of a town, especially as it is flanked by a church tower on one side and a monument on the other. The forms of the conventional libraries do not harmonize very well, as a rule, with the old types of architecture, but a change is coming about in this respect, and while it is too late to modify very much the general impression, since so

OSSIPEE LAKE

A SACO FIELD ROAD—OSSIPEE

WILTON WATERS

A CHOCORUA CURVE

many libraries have been erected, still we may hope here and there to see, as in this instance, a departure from the inharmonious structures so generally found.

Westmoreland, Canaan, Franklin, and Conway all possess features of interest in their village centers which give a certain dignity and character.

In the ancient day the English settler, so different from the French in his habits, cared and did little for the architectural center of his town. He assisted in the erection of the church, being in the first place taxed for that purpose. Beyond that, large families and a busy life left the settler without much leisure or sense of need of any municipal structures. Even the church edifice was often used for town-meetings. In other cases the town house was a combination of school and hall.

CLOUD EFFECTS

IN THE latter part of this volume (from page 236 on) we have secured a considerable number of cloud effects with lake or mountain. Perhaps the beauty of the country is half in its atmosphere. The changing lights, caused by the change in atmospheric moisture, give aspects to nature that are at times wholly startling. The dense, yellow-green light coming through a heavy haze, brings out every growth with a relief and a shading quite distinct from the garish noon-day lights when the world is least attractive. The year 1923 has been rather remarkable for its wonderful cloud display. We recently recorded an expanse of sky which in every part was broken up into even masses of white cloud, small, irregular parallelograms arranged in ranks like soldiers, so that the entire heavens must have held one or two thousand of them. This was a display such as the writer at least had never seen, and to the eye of the farmer may have suggested a potato field with the irregular hills after harvesting the crop. To a textile designer it may have suggested a scheme of colored fabric on a blue ground with irregular white masses in symmetrical rows.

This was really a modified " mackerel " sky, but far more extensive and beautiful. This year has also been fruitful in those skies which show in the background stratified masses of cloud of a dull-gray hue, and in front of them two other strata, one consisting of scattered, small, formless wisps and the stratum in the foreground consisting of small, smoke-colored clouds. This scheme of superimposed strata affords perhaps the most telling display.

We have been reminded this year of the marvelous fidelity with which Winkle in his Cathedrals must have studied the clouds to secure his wonderful wood-cuts, which in their variety and beauty seem to exceed any similar collection of pictures of cloud-masses. We have also observed this year, as we are beginning to record these beautiful shapes, a great many indefinable combinations that change in form and color, so that in the course of a day two or three score different effects are produced. In a level land, such as are some of the broader meadows of New England, these cloud-masses are the chief distinction of the landscape, and when they are absent the scene is somewhat tame. The prairies owe to their clouds, therefore, most of their beauty, but in a mountainous country the effect of the clouds, massing over the hills, and casting their reflections in the lakes or over the forests, is an endless moving-picture of a beauty transcending any other feature of country life. The delicate blues, seen through the breaks in cumulus clouds before the rich-colored effects of evening come on, are to our mind as entrancing as any natural phenomenon.

When we consider the extent of the background on which sky effects are painted, their color and the exquisite forms by which they array themselves at even distances, and when we recall that all the effects in shape and color of cloud are the results of dust and moisture, the infinite variety and the glory of the resultant combinations is marvelous. There is a series of fixed laws regarding the height at which clouds are suspended in proportion to their weight and the varying weights of the atmosphere, and then, combined with these fixed laws, there is the variation of the winds, sometimes fierce and sometimes almost ceasing, at times steady and

CHOCORUA DAISIES

AN OSSIPEE SICKLE

A WOOD IN JUNE—ROCKINGHAM COUNTY

BENDING BOUGHS—CHOCORUA ROAD

again affording a ruffling or wrinkled effect, by what means we can scarcely understand.

The color of clouds is also influenced by their density or their mass. By one law or another, by one apparent whim or another of the moving air, there have been assembled and dispersed again as many myriad canvases of splendor across the sky as there have been days since first clouds rose above the earth. And in all this infinite movement, this parade-ground of azure, there have been no precise duplications of form since the beginning of time. We never see two clouds alike.

When we attempt to predict a meaning of cloud movements we are also baffled. In certain regions, as in New England, when they move from the west we look for fine weather, but in the period of thunder-storms even this prediction is precarious. Where is the man who can tell when the sky induced by an east wind will break? This same east wind has been, since America was settled, the butt of more jokes and curses than any other natural phenomenon. We are as far as ever from being able to predict anything of its continuance.

The effect upon moisture-laden atmosphere, of the sun breaking through rain and forming a bow was sufficiently striking to be used as the climax and the completion of the deluge story. We have, before now, succeeded in securing pictures of rainbows, but the coloring was not attractive. In fact men nowhere fail so completely as when they try to paint the skies. The work there is done on a scale and with a subtlety which transcends all possible efforts of ours. It is as if the scheme of things was designed so that every humble human being might possess paintings surpassing the canvases of the masters in the halls of the nabobs of the earth. There is a beautiful and serene democracy in the manner in which cloud majesties are arrayed. The babe first coming to look at the out-of-door world is summoned to admire the panorama of the sky. It is natural that in the sky, clothed with the terrors or the daintinesses of clouds, the gods should have been thought to have had their abode. Even

[Text continued on page 149.]

A SYRINGA DOOR

Home —
With its dear syringa bowers
Of star-like flowers —
Not solemn and grand,
Groomed by a gardener's hand
Into formal cones and balls,
Like the proud, bright shrubs that stand
Outside the entrances of marble halls —
With liveried servants!

But syringas —
Just friendly, simple, and sweet
As they bend to meet
Above the old home door
In garlands green
And lustrous gold and white;
Tenderly waiting, as a sweetheart might,
All fragrant and serene,
Beside the flag-stone steps —
A sweetheart fair,
With buds and blossoms in her hair
By the soft breezes stirred;
And whirring, darting, glistening there,
A jewelled hummingbird!

Syringa doors —
With their little, friendly blossom-stars
Gleaming through memory's dusk —
Welcoming wanderers far and wide
Back to New Hampshire's fire-side!

MILDRED HOBBS

THE LAKE LANE—OSSIPEE

SYRINGA DOOR—CHESTER

THE WANALANCET ROAD

PEACE ON THE SACO—OSSIPEE

A CHESTER GARDEN

in the Christian scheme God is in His heaven. The sky is the most elo-
quent of books, readable in all languages. Wherever wars go on in the
torn planet on which we live, the continuance under law and beauty of the
sky-glory goes on, untouched by our quarrels, unmarred by the soiling of
our reeking centuries. So strange is it that the most varying, the lightest
and the least definable aspect of the world is the most permanent, the
most beautiful, and the altogether stimulating call to faith.

But the clouds have secrets for us, the first chapter of which, recorded
by Franklin, has been sought forever since. The electrical energy con-
stantly generated by the clouds is probably ample for the largest possible
needs of civilization. Amid the various theories advanced to account for
the building up of electrical energy in the skies, we at least know that it

is not lacking in quantity, if we ever learn how to call it all down, or even an appreciable part of it. We can then easily change the face of the earth to something vastly better than at present. Meantime the cloud-masses form to shield us from the heat of summer, to vary the monotony of life, to stimulate our thought and to carry forth doubtless various other more important purposes. To a person of artistic instincts and a natural lover of beauty, the clouds are sometimes almost the only con-solation amid the dreariness of the cities and on the barren plains. The sky is the dependable hope of the artist. He knows that soon it will furnish him a fresh model more beautiful than he can follow, and yet alluring him ever to make the stimulating effort.

THE PERSISTENCE OF LIFE

IN NEW HAMPSHIRE Lichen (p. 207) we are reminded of the amazing persistency of life shown by the lichen. After a long drought, when the lichen is dry and brown and apparently dead, lying between the hot sun and the hot stone behind it, one would think there was no possible help for it. But at the first rain its soft greens reappear, and it begins to grow again. It is the most beautiful instance in nature, of which we are aware, of the persistency, under apparently impossible con-ditions, of life. The lichen certainly cannot get anything from the rock. How can it get its green substance from the air and how can it continue in life under conditions so adverse? It forms in dells, like that in the picture before us, a very decorative feature. It gives individuality to each stone. It speaks with a more certain voice than any other vegetation the power of life to fix itself in the world. We have spoken before of the beginning of life by the breaking down of the rock. Here is the life before the rock is broken down, because the lichen subsists apparently equally well on the hard granite boulder. Thus we see that it is not necessary for us to suppose the breaking down of the rock before some

A CONTOOCOOK PINE — HENNIKER

THE ISLAND — FRANKLIN

BENDING BOUGHS — SACO RIVER

A BANK SIDE HOMESTEAD — FRANKLIN

sort of life began. The survival of the wheat seed after centuries and perhaps thousands of years has often been cited as a cause of long persistent life, but to our mind the instance before us is even more remarkable. The manner in which the sequoia in California continues on from millennium to millennium is a marvel which we never weary of remembering. Some would even go so far as to say that germs of a sort of life may have come to us in meteorites, the thick dust from them entering the soil. At any rate, it is certain that plants, and we ourselves, eating those plants, live in some part on meteorites, and into our physical system has entered material from the universe outside the earth. We are not such provincials after all! In the data which we have secured regarding atoms and ether we have some reason to suppose that elements from the sun enter into the leaf of plants. If so, we are the children of the sun and stars in a more literal sense than the poet would suppose.

Doubtless to beings of a higher order than ourselves, we may look like lichen on a rock, so far as the present state of our development is concerned. Yet it need not be altogether to our discredit that we are no better than we are. It seems to us that the lichen is doing very well to live at all. When the diabolic germs that attack men are so numerous that they have not even been counted, although we are working on the job all the time, we are doing very well to be here at all. It is true that some animals, like the elephant and the turtle, are said to outstrip us in length of life. But who wants to be a turtle or even an elephant? We know, also, that the flea can jump one hundred and fifty times its length, and the cricket on the hearth, when a child attempts to tickle it, gets ahead astonishingly. Yet we prefer our human status. The lichen is a most encouraging plant. It is the silent and continuous reminder that life keeps going on. Students of disease tell us that it is easily possible that some plague may destroy every human creature. We refuse to be disturbed. We have lived here in a man or manlike form for a million years or so, and we are still growing stronger.

It is true that some animals can bear being frozen and perhaps even boiled, and recover their vitality. In all these instances in which lower orders of life seem to surpass us we have the consoling thought that intelligence can steer us clear of being boiled or frozen, and in one way or another our affection or intelligence or their combination come to the rescue and keep mankind alive. If a thing as frail as the lichen can persist, why may we not persist? If the ferns in the foreground in this picture can be so beautiful why may not even a commercial age learn to love beauty for itself alone and to cultivate it without a thought of ledgers?

SECRET PLACES

THE Hidden Fountain (p. 211) may serve to remind us that the nooks and corners of the world are favorable for dreams. A gentle pessimist may hint that they who dream must first sleep, and that the bucolic mind has not been notable as a source of literature or invention. Not so fast! Do we not find the deepest thinkers retiring either to the mountains or to the lonely shore or to a secluded country nook? Because we find highly intelligent men at the centers of human life, we should infer not that they derive their intellectuality from the propinquity of so much noise and distraction, but that it is in such centers that their intellectual powers are most needed. It may be true that we cannot point to a continuous abode of great geniuses in remote nooks. Yet to such nooks they went either occasionally or for considerable periods. The bird forages widely for its young. So we humans wander far to bring back something for those who remain at home. As the bird goes afield, so must the man. The wealth is not all in the cities and it never will be. Some one has wittily said that the farmer accumulates until he has enough, on selling out, to remove to the city, and there he goes on accumulating until he has enough to buy a country place.

A healthful life cannot be lived either at a hidden fountain of Egeria or amid teeming millions. Interchange of residence is ideal for intellect as well as for the body. As Kipling dwelt at Brattleboro and Emerson at

THE SACO AT PLAY — TAMWORTH

DANIEL WEBSTER BIRTHPLACE — FRANKLIN

A NEW HAMPSHIRE BORDER — CHOCORUA

A CRESCENT SHORE — HILLSBORO

THE ANCIENT TOWN POUND, DURHAM

Concord and many a genius in the New Hampshire hills for summers, or even years at a time, it is apparent that freshness of mind is secured by a country residence. Many fear that they will go to seed in the country. That depends upon the person concerned. Doubtless there are many minds that soon break down in the city.

We recall a notable public speaker who never could do well until he had two cups of strong coffee. He would have been a far abler man could he have marshaled his intellectual forces without the coffee. Doubtless, sleepy minds require the city. Minds weary from continual agitation need the country. There they may drink at the fountain of Egeria; there they may wade on the silvery strands; there they may cut the names of their beloved ones on the beech boles. Indeed, it is quite apparent to one who has looked about on the country roads that this is the principal purpose of the beech tree. In the country, men may lie where May snowflakes from the apple trees drop on their nervous noses, and lull them to sleep.

Of course, the country is the remedy for over-stimulated people. We are curiously so built that cases of insanity, however, are very common among solitary persons or those who dwell apart fom other human habitations. This insanity results from introspection or brooding or longing for the life outside. Thus it appears that the country man needs the city occasionally, and this need he may now satisfy by new means of conveyance, and the newspaper keeps him in immediate touch with the thought of the world. Thus everything that assists transportation may be used to keep down the numbers in our asylums for the insane and increase our product of good literature.

The secret nooks of the country are particularly desirable, say, for a couple of months in the year. In those nooks no telephones are allowed. The really big man can bear this because the resources in himself are sufficient and more than sufficient to keep him stirred up. He is in the country to rest. Of course, those who go into the country for other reasons do not seek the hidden fountains.

If one, however, whose head is weary fords the stream (p. 227) for some hours and sees no human folly, but instead the silent peaks, and hears no human noises, but listens only to the plaintive babble of the brook, the results cannot be other than good.

We are accustomed to hearing men say they have no time for these things. Such a remark indicates after all a mediocre mind. The greatest minds know how to take time. It is only the half-great who are always hurried.

Who could not profitably spend three hours under the maples (p. 228) and, with his fingers between the leaves of an old volume of Washington Irving, lounge on the green bank and think better thoughts than at home? To be sure, he always wants the book. It will help him to sleep, especially if it is a good book. The poor book only irritates him. We have learned that to think quietly along one chain of thought is soothing if we must not think too alertly. In this the book helps us. Thus at home, if we

THREE SISTERS ROAD—ANTRIM

A SACO MEDLEY—OSSIPEE

A LITTLE BRIDGE — HILLSBORO

A NEW HAMPSHIRE ELM — ANTRIM

toss distracted between a hundred ideas, a good book steadies the mind and finally soothes it and induces sleep.

We knew of an occasion when a somewhat unnerved man, very fond of good public speaking, went sound asleep when he listened to a notable orator. Perhaps the orator did not know that the sleeper paid him the highest compliment!

SOCIETY IN THE COUNTRY

ONE of the objections to country life has been the alleged loss of the social features enjoyed in town. At Cornish that loss has been remedied by the gathering, within short compass, of a large number of persons of taste, or those engaged in literary and artistic pursuits. It is natural enough that birds of a feather should get together. In the attractive scenery of Cornish together with a large number of acres susceptible of cultivation there is found an adequate setting for a neighborhood colony.

Conditions are so utterly changed by motors that it is no longer necessary to be nearer than twenty miles to a good neighborhood. Yet it has been found pleasing to keep among friends the adjoining farms. Desirable neighborhoods seem to be no less desirable, among fashionable people at least, now that quick and easy transportation is general. It is curious that in spite of the ease of getting about the difference of five miles makes all the possible difference in the supposed desirability of country estates and in the valuations placed on lands.

Where several like-minded people get together in the country they really see each other very much more than in town. Also, though they have books and their own intellectual resources they are free from certain obnoxious features of town life. They, therefore, find country life very favorable for literary and artistic productions, and it has become common to find studios in the country located in immediate view of the scenes to be painted.

Cornish is within view of the dominating peak of the region which, however, is in Vermont, i.e., Ascutney. Windsor, also in Vermont, forms the principal railway connection of the region and Windsor is in itself the abode of not a few persons notable in national life for their literary achievements.

Prediction is proverbially dangerous but the writer feels sure that certain of the townships south of Cornish, notably Westmoreland, will, before many years pass, also become a favorite summer residence and social center, though it is now in the quiet, distinctly unexploited stage. Its contour is most pleasing, its center at the old village green, whose church and parsonage form such attractive features, is altogether a desirable neighborhood.

We have previously noted the social center of Dublin. Of course, Bethlehem owing to its being a resort for hay fever sufferers is also incidentally an important social center. Walpole has its social features and a somewhat extensive list of country attractions. Peterboro, in the vicinity of Dublin, is nevertheless an independent social center of some importance. Outdoor professional theatricals are carried forward in its neighborhood. Pike has a good number of like-minded individuals who have made it sought for their particular fellowship. The districts where there is no hotel are preferred by the cottagers since hotel life brings into the country certain town features which the cottager seeks to avoid.

Thus Cornish and the purely social centers where hotels are very secondary are perhaps most sought by those who want homes of their own.

We may presume that in process of time, as like seeks like, various neighborhoods in New Hampshire will become more and more distinctly marked, as notable each one for a certain sort of resident devoted as the case may be to art, to authorship, to athletics and to fashionable society.

LATE RIVER LIGHTS — NEW BOSTON

A VILLAGE MEETING HOUSE — HANCOCK

A DUBLIN CLUSTER

THE CALL OF THE FOREST—ANTRIM

A DURHAM DOOR

THE ROMANCE OF THE SCHOOL HOUSE

A GOOD deal has been said in political references and otherwise of the old red school house and some of it has been wise and some of it has been foolish. We mean that it is an easy subject to talk about and when the politician wants something to say he is likely to glorify the school as appealing to the largest number of people.

We have called the picture (p. 279) a School House Romance because there is so much about it that sets us tingling with memories. This edifice close to the center of Westmoreland has now been abandoned. The main portion is brick and the old porch and the shed are of wood. Above still remains a forked support for the school bell which has vanished. The large chimney, the affectionate vines, the overhanging trees, the lady's lace growing up to the open door and even about the door-step, all assist in a composition such that this edifice may be said to embody the romance of the country school.

Of course we know that the country school was altogether what the teacher made it. If she was competent and had character the school was a fine institution. We often forget that institutions are good or evil not owing to the bricks or stones which enter into them but owing to their leadership. We have had reason to know during the past thirty years that a good many country schools were little better than none and we could omit the word " country " from this statement and not shade the truth.

We are always being misled by new names and new combinations just as if the same persons would not function in one place practically in the same way as in another. This old school house doubtless had those leaders within its walls who sent out a sturdy, aspiring young life instructed in the great basal ideas which are the glory of America. But we remember from country experiences that often the teacher lacked force or knowledge or character and was held in contempt by the neighborhood as well as by the scholars until some particularly glaring instance of inefficiency drove her out, for generally the teachers of these schools were women and it was generally best that they should be.

The gathering together of pupils in a large edifice has no advantages whatever unless the teachers are to be of the right kind. It is true that the modern system of gathering the pupils by a public conveyance has some advantages. Again it has disadvantages as children are in danger of for-

SILENCE AND SHADOW — HANCOCK

A NEW HAMPSHIRE OCTOBER

ELM BEND—HILLSBORO COUNTY

PETERBORO WATERS

getting how to walk and there is plenty of time when they grow up to forget that. We know instances where pupils are riding a quarter of a mile to school, and where a little flurry of snow is sufficient to intermit the pursuit of knowledge.

The author's first experience of school was at the age of four years in a remote country town of Maine. There was no village. We think every private edifice in town was a farm house. The snows were sometimes of very great depth, but we do not remember that the school house was ever closed a day during term time. In the case of desperate storms the farmers turned out to open the roads and help the children through, but a foot and a half of snow was not considered worth bothering about. It it true that this is an extreme instance, and we remember, with a sad pang, an aunt some eighty years ago, and a cousin, the niece of that aunt, some forty years ago, who became permanently insane from attempting to attend school through snow storms. There is, of course, reason in all things, and extreme exposure of any kind is not advocated. Nevertheless, we maintain that the tendency of the day is toward too much coddling of the scholar.

The old red school house had nothing in the way of equipment except a black board. As a rule there was not even a globe, — a very grave omission, since nothing assists so much in helping the pupil to orient himself. Nevertheless the children learned to spell which they do not do now, and they learned the physical bounds of their state and nation and got their bearings in general. Education had to do wholly with the head and confined itself to essentials. Our schools as now conducted may be said to paraphrase a well-known remark: they can get on without the necessities but not without the luxuries.

How would the idea strike Americans who love the old red school house to get the edifice which we are particularly considering into their hands, form a little society for its restoration and preservation and equip it with the books and the stove and the wood pile such as it had at first? A little old school house like this might become a kind of local museum of patriotism, of memory and of sentiment, and might serve to embody for the coming generation the idea of the country school as it was. Here is an edifice that nobody seems to want and which the town has ignored and abandoned, although it is still substantial enough in general. Some dear spinster who embodies the finer characteristics of the school mistress of the past generations might be installed in summer to show visitors what the country school is like. Obviously various ramifying ideas might grow out from this proposal and such an old school house might serve as a local center. Why shouldn't it house the country library? Why should it not be an information bureau for summer guests, as a center for old home weeks and old home summers, as a landmark and a beacon, or as an example of the great American idea? Meantime as we wade through the lady's lace and the seeding grasses we sit on the worn door step where so many little feet, some glad and some rebellious, have gone in and out. Where are they now? Some of them led faithfully on the battlefields of France; some of them walk in stately places; some of them have gone down the strand and into the waters of the sea whose farther shore is invisible. We come upon their names here and there in the country churchyard. Without genius but with a sweet humanity they were faithful friends.

We meet others on strange quests, some good, some evil. But when we mention the old school house a mellowing humanity diffuses itself over their countenances. It is the touch which makes us all kin. The escapades and red letter days of childhood come back.

We do not enough preserve the old scenes and the old memories. They give continuity and dignity to life and take away from it the sense of disconnectedness now too common.

What is America without memories? It is true that it is easy to deify the past, and unhappily it is easy to deify an evil past. A great deal that is old ought to vanish. It has outlived its day, and perhaps never ought to have been. But without the sweeter and more endearing memories and those that make for kindliness and brotherhood, any world, ancient or modern, would be a hell.

A DUBLIN CURVE

HUMPTY DUMPTY BROOK—NELSON

WAVERING SHADOWS—HILLSBORO

THE CINCINNATI CHAPTER, EXETER

IN THE CHANGING COUNTRY

WE ARE accustomed to the changes in cities so that no American
city of any size knows itself as it was a generation since. Its
sky outlines, its streets, its edifices, its customs have been almost completely
changed. We have been used, however, to think of the country as more
conservative. We fear this habit of men is not based on the facts. On
the Isles of Shoals for instance where was once a large and thrifty com-
munity of self-supporting persons, there is very little left of the old life.
On one isle in particular which supported hundreds of people there may
be said to be nothing left. An almost equally sweeping statement could
be made in relation to a great many New Hampshire communities on the
main land. The trends of modern life have swept them away. Here

[*Text continued on page* 177.]

CREAM AND GOLD

The charming roads of Antrim,
In gay October dress,
Are like the roads of paradise —
All golden loveliness!

Aglow with shafts of sunlight
That filter through the trees;
And burnished with the birchen leaves,
Down-drifting in the breeze.

And O, the leaves are yellow
As pointed drops of sun;
Their gaily fluttering canopies
The fairies must have spun!

And clustered trunks, reflecting
The glory overhead,
Stand creamy white along the way,
With slender boughs outspread.

The old stone walls are gilded!
Their mica is ablaze!
And all the fields and mountains lie
Beneath a shining haze.

What splendid flying pennons
October days unfold
Along the charming Antrim roads —
The roads of cream and gold!

CREAM AND GOLD—ANTRIM

THE NORTH BRANCH — CONTOOCOOK RIVER

MONADNOCK FROM JAFFREY

and there on a hill top will be an old meeting house where none meet any more. Many a road has its abandoned houses and farms going back to the wilderness. The supposition that those who dwelt here, or their children, have bettered their condition, is by no means always true. The vague unrest which has always been a feature of the Nordic peoples is a sufficient explanation why many of them have moved into cities or into the west. It is easy to trace many of the families of New Hampshire to regions where only one crop may be raised at a profit. It is easy to trace them to neighborhoods more remote, or more lacking the uplift of the best elements of society, than those regions which they have left. Or we may find them buried in the smoky or crowded quarters of great cities, where they have lost their more valuable characteristics. It would be a serious mistake to presume that any farm house or any farm is abandoned merely because those who once inhabited and delved here are now doing better.

The exploring and moving instinct is sufficient to account for at least half of the migrations. Considered broadly there are certain benefits from migrations in the way of stimulating human ideas and of developing distant regions, even arid regions. But it is always a misfortune when all the people move on. We were speaking recently of the old red school house. We believe the very next farm to the school house is what was once a good and well located dwelling now abandoned. There was good land, plenty of water, wood and a reasonable access to market. There was a fine outlook and such airs as have fostered centenarians. But no one cared to keep up the old house. Where children had teemed and a vital country life was found, now all is still. Some who went out from here found themselves in a land where the mere materials and patching together of a makeshift shack cost them more than they would now be asked to pay for the old farm and its edifice. They are in a far land but not in a better land. There is economically, esthetically and romantically a far better occupation in putting this old house to rights and in redeeming its old acres than in some far wandering where mere trans-

[*Text continued on page* 181.]

BRIDGE BOWS

Under a bridge in Hillsboro
A painting hangs in an oval frame —
Bright yellows from the lily-cups,
Soft greens from sloping fields beyond
And tall reeds lush along the shore —
All painted with a faithful brush
On crystal of the Contoocook,
And set within bridge bows of stone.

Among the valleys and the hills
Are little roads with thank-you-ma'ams
And grassy ridges, dotted o'er
With clover blooms and buttercups,
Like two long ribbons winding on,
With here and there a little bridge
Above the babbling of a brook.
And these we love, whose rustic logs
Pound with the thud of horses' hoofs
And jolly rumble of the wheels!

Beneath the little bridges, too,
Are miniatures in wooden frames —
A streak of rainbow leaping through
The spray of tiny waterfalls!
A lizard, basking on a rock
Beside a crimson river-bud!
And all through Nature's gallery
Where brooks and streams and rivers course,
Hang paintings rare, within bridge bows.

MILDRED HOBBS

BRIDGE BOWS—HILLSBORO COUNTY

THE BIRCH FRAME—CHOCORUA

MONADNOCK FROM A GARDEN—JAFFREY

portation entails an expense that would finance all the work required at the old farm.

We are assured in our minds, through observation and experience, that there are communities of considerable size where no one knows or cares for good domestic architecture. Somebody ought to write a book on the Lost Arts in America. We are so constituted that the ordinary intelligence cannot grasp many departments of learning. Perhaps the modern man is better informed in some respects than was his father or his grandfather. But if he does not know a good house when he sees it or good acres or a good location or a good aim, has he not exchanged good knowledge for bad?

We are eager to see these New Hampshire hills touched by the spirit of progress which knows how to build upon a mellow and strong past. The first essential to this desirable end is to cease to despise the ways of the past. We must learn to love the ground and its walls. We must again feel the moral asset that goes with substantial building. We must recognize the right of roadside trees to live, and rise in indignant and effectual protest against their general demolition. We must learn to believe in the human family as the divinely ordained unit of society. Particularly we require to know how to build upon the past without destroying it. As we often see a good old edifice relegated to the background on the farm, and a new and tawdry dwelling built in front of it, so we may extend the analogy to life in general. Many have considered that they should build wholly anew and break utterly with the past, using none of its foundations, turning their back to its mellow richness and warmth and thinking that history is "bunk." The finest civilizations are those which develop rather than destroy. The best farms, the best dwellings, the best roads and the best characters are those that are built up with modern modifications out of the old foundations, but conserving all that is worth while.

By what possible process of reasoning are institutions which have had a

[*Text continued on page 185.*]

FROM SHADOW COVE

We're off, little skiff of mine,
For a-fishing we would go,
With a rod as light as a feather,
And a heart as free as the air!
Glide off from the sandy shore
To the dreamy spot we know,
Where many a day out yonder
We have left all trouble and care.

Drift light where the lily pads float
In the quiet shade of the grove,
For it's here that we love to linger
To the pure delight of the soul;
Where the pickerel hide in the weeds
And sleep in the nooks of the cove —
But we go where the gamey bass play,
We're off to the secret shoal!

And the oar-locks softly click
To the rhythmic dip of the oars,
And the silence gathers about us
With the whirring song of the reel!
But I turn your bow at last
To the shadowed curve of the shores
With a treasure of glistening beauties
In the willow depths of the creel!

MILDRED HOBBS

SHADOW COVE—HANCOCK

"SKY PLANE" OF ECHO LAKE — FRANCONIA

MONADNOCK FROM THORNDIKE POND

stamp of centuries or millenniums of approval now assumed to be worthless? Of course we know that this contempt for the past arises not from rationality but from the lack of it. It arises from thoughtlessness and ignorance and a roving foot. Particularly it arises from a lack of the value of history, so that every generation is doing over again the foolish things that were found to be foolish so long ago, and throwing aside the good things of other generations found to be good so long ago. Of course life must change very greatly. The ideal man is not he who throws himself wholly into modern life, assuming its inventions and processes to be the whole of existence. Neither is the ideal man he who rummages and putters over antiquities and merely dwells in the good old days, which for the most part are imaginary. But the ideal character is he who knows how to adapt the present to the past and to avoid the loss of half a million years' experience in half a decade of modern conceit. The enrichment of life consists in additions to that good which has been demonstrated and found beautiful and practical. Progress is not merely leaving our baggage and rushing on. It consists in crowning history with its own lessons and in incorporating all good, whatever its date, in the fuller and more abounding present day personality.

UP TUCKERMAN'S RAVINE

A GENERATION ago the writer made one of a party of five youths to journey from Fryeburg to the summit of Mount Washington. We started bright and early in the old carryall, and drove up the Glen to the point of departure on foot. Leaving our vehicle in a stable we packed on our backs food and blankets, and began the ascent. The day was hot. None of us had ever made the climb. We were, after long and close study, rather inapt for brisk exertion. Picking our way among the rocks we met with no untoward difficulty, but the steady pull of lifting ourselves and the packs was very noticeable before we reached the summit. There, after exploring some time, we looked about for a possible shelter for the night.   An old railroad shed served our purpose well enough.   After we had consumed a good half of our rations we turned in and shivered through a long night.   Be sure that it was before sunrise that we rose from our uncomfortable quarters and went out to enjoy the glories of the upper air.   Lips covered with fever sores, from the intense heat and the long pull, were one of the consequences.   We got little beside.   We were too young, too unobserving.   We remember that effort as one which might have yielded records of value.   We passed by, that was all.

SOME NEW HAMPSHIRE DWELLINGS

THE interior of the front door in the Warner hall (p. 16) is an interesting example of how the thing was done in the best houses in the early part of the eighteenth century.   This house is thoroughly elegant, the panels running to the ceilings in more than one room.   The front door, however, is made double with solid plain back as was the custom. On the front, the door is paneled, and one would never suspect the scheme by which our ancestors secured strength and avoided the wood's habit of buckling.   The catch of this door is curiously braced sidewise, being the only one of the sort that we have seen.   The ancient moose antlers were a gift to Captain MacPhaedris from the Indians.   In the hallway as one ascends the stairs there is an exceedingly quaint series of paintings on the plaster, the main theme being the sacrifice of Isaac.   In the distance there are two servants holding the horses.   They are dressed out in the style of the period when the house was built, in perukes and long tail coats. Farther down the stairs there seems to be a kind of version of Hannah's Child.   A dog is scaring away an eagle from the cradle by the side of which the mother sits spinning.   At the turn of the stairs at the other side is a man on horseback who is done about life-size, and altogether in profile except the face which is turned squarely toward us.   This painting

A BIRCH APPROACH—GREYSTONE LODGE

A FOREST BOWL—HILL

ROCK BOUND ISLES OF SHOALS

is the most curious and fascinating of anything of the sort with which we have been made familiar.

The lights over the front doors, which in this period were never in the fan shape, were often if not generally bull's eyes. The supposition of the layman is, of course, that the bull's eyes were choice pieces especially selected. The fact is that the bull's eye was the nubbin or remnant left after the blower had finished his finer work, and it was used expressly for such places as this to admit light without permitting a clear image to appear.

There is a dainty door (p. 17) with a window over which hang vines. It has been delicately done by Miss E. Blanche Brown from our photograph. This house is opposite the John Paul Jones house of which we show no pictures though it is thoroughly worthy just as are a hundred others in Portsmouth. We have, however, pictures of equally good houses. This house, named in honor of the great founder of the American navy, it is understood was the boarding place of Jones during a large part of his residence in Portsmouth while he was fitting out the *Ranger*. The Historical Society which has it in charge has been the recipient within a short time of most beautiful and important objects. The location of the house is ideal for the purpose and it is worthy also of its contents. Nevertheless, we cannot but feel that it is almost an error to store these collections in inflammable dwellings. We speak feelingly of the matter because we have had such collections in dwellings of wood and even at the present time we are facing the question of whether articles of historic and perhaps unique artistic value should be stored where there is danger of fire. Presumably it is this feeling which is making us all look toward the museum as the final recipient of articles of this character.

The door of the Coleman house (p. 25), while not especially elaborate, is one of the finer examples of the period. The door itself could scarcely be original but we believe all the other parts are original. The doorhead is exceptional in this respect, it has been so carefully painted that the condition is almost as perfect as when new.

LEBANON ARCHES

MIDSUMMER HOLLYHOCKS

NEWFOUND LAKE

We show the Richter and the Warner doors (p. 33).   The Richter door is an interesting example of the iron post and chain style in connection with the front steps and the fence, and is quite typical.   The relieving arches over the windows are also excellent, and this house while not open to the public except through the courtesy of the owners has much of interest in the interior.

The Warner door also, while not especially elaborate, has been so well taken care of that we can see very particularly what the builder intended. It will be observed that the builder had some difficulty in locating the knocker on paneled doors.   It was a question whether the knocker should be placed on one side of the center, on a stile, or on a rail, the lower part to strike in the panel as in this instance.   Both methods were used.   The keyholes to these doors were often mere round openings for the insertion of a key without wards.

In the City of Paris Paper (p. 35) we have a finely preserved example in the town of Walpole, of landscape paper.   It is in the Knapp house.

The Jackson house (p. 41) is regarded as the oldest dwelling in Portsmouth.   It is a pity that it could not be restored to something like its original condition.   Of course the leanto on the face of the gable could not have been original because a window appears on the gable, the top of which only is now in sight.   Nevertheless, this leanto is old and interesting.   The rear leanto, the extension of the main roof, is one of the best known instances in which the eaves and the earth come close together. This is partly, of course, owing to the contour of the ground, such that a stone wall constitutes the back of this leanto.   This house has a good many merits of a typical character, and it does not stand at all alone in this respect, but we are of the opinion that almost any house anterior to 1700 is worth preserving.   The view in front of this dwelling is particularly fascinating, sloping down as it does to Christian Shore.   If some of the out-buildings of the next property were cleared away and the balance masked by a small clump of evergreens, the outlook would be perfect. The author has sometimes been tempted to purchase and restore this house but he thinks he has done more than his duty in such restorations.

There is another dwelling in Portsmouth which we cannot show owing to its location, but which also richly merits attention. It is called the First Wentworth House, and is on Manning Street. The porch is recent and the wonderful old heavily paneled doors of the earliest type have been removed down stairs, and lost or destroyed, but up stairs the original doors are in place.

This dwelling is unique in some respects among the very earliest houses. Its stairway is composed of oak spiral spindles, the solitary instance that we have encountered in America of oak used in this connection with a spiral. We speak with reserve because no one knows what may be discovered at any time and no one knows what someone else has already discovered. These facts, however, generally get about after a little while, and the sum total of general knowledge on such subjects is usually a very large percentage of the total private knowledge. This stair rail continues into the very attic and even goes along by the side of the chimney there. It affords entrance to a room which has a true, though small hammer beam, the only instance we have noted in this country. The interior of the house is deceptive at first. The room on the right was originally like that on the left, — one great space from front to back of the house. That is to say the main house is only one room deep down stairs. A temporary partition now exists in the room on the right, on the side of the beholder, running directly into the ancient fireplace. With the removal of this partition one would have two marvelous rooms. This house is claimed to date as early as 1670. We have not been able to verify this date but there are many features which indicate the first period of American dwellings.

The leanto running the entire length of the rear of the house and having a room opening from the kitchen at each end is as interesting as any other part of the dwelling. Its fine fireplace and old sheathed

LEBANON BIRCHES

LEBANON WATERS

THE RUMNEY RANGE

paneling are of the best character. To be sure one does not get the depth secured in a great kitchen but there is a cosiness secured in a small room.

The main room on the left of the beholder is fine in respect to its paneling. Some owner being ashamed of it carefully pasted canvas strips over the hollows of the panel work and then papered all over. On the removal of this vandalism one would arrive at a very dignified and satisfactory interior. The summer-beam is very large indeed. We infer that a great many dwellings built in the latter part of the sevententh century were paneled somewhat after their erection when paneling became so fashionable from 1720 on.

The location of this house while against it, nevertheless could be made pleasing, by clearing away the rubbish up to the adjoining street on the open end and making an approach from that quarter and laying out an old-fashioned garden.

The gable is one of the most interesting, being sharp according to the almost uniform custom of the period. This dwelling is supposed to have been lived in by the first Wentworth whose application for a license to keep a public house is on file well back in the seventeenth century, and it is presumed that this house was used for the purpose of an inn.

Bowered in woodbine, the cottage on the west bank of Lake Winnepesaukee (p. 43) shows a house going back to nature. The beauty of the effect is very much enhanced by the elm in the rear. If these walls had been brick or stone, the vine would not have done so much damage. Even so, in England it is claimed that vine growths, especially the ivy, injure walls, insinuating their minute tendrils into the mortar and distintegrating it in time. Most owners are willing to take their chances. If the work is done with cement mortar of fine consistency it is probable that no injury would result from vines.

Another Portsmouth door with the scrolled iron hand rail combining with the fence at the foot (p. 47) is the semicircular front with posts.

[*Text continued on page* 201.]

MUSICAL STONES, FRANCONIA

Far in the hills,
In the shadow of the trees,
Close by the pines
Where the water falls are foaming —
Here let me dream
In the balsam-laden breeze —
Here voices call
Through forest-gloaming.

Long have they sung
To the dreamers by the way —
Smooth, sparkling rocks
Where the rivulets are falling;
White jetting streams
And the murmur of the spray —
All through the years,
Ceaselessly calling.

Lull me to rest,
Tinkling music of the stones —
Soothe me to sleep
With the rush of waters swinging!
Blend with my dreams
In your gentle, treble tones,
Rhythmic and sweet —
Lullabies singing!

Mildred Hobbs

MUSICAL STONES—FRANCONIA

MASCOMA LAKE — ENFIELD

TUFTED WATERS — RAYMOND

This was the favorite scheme in the last quarter of the eighteenth century, particularly the latter part of that quarter.

The old Rockingham church (p. 76) is remarkable for the great number of lights in the windows and also for its door in the side which is an early type, though this edifice itself is not so ancient as some in Massachusetts. It is, nevertheless, much cherished by the people of Rockingham who hold annual celebrations here. Standing as it does against the sky it is a monument of the days when so many went to church that a large gallery was necessary.

Portsmouth from the Harbor (p. 87) shows the town before the great new bridge was erected and is a typical outline of an early New England city with the quaint roof lines and the belfry.

Enclosed gardens are somehow the solitary instance in which fences seem to be desirable. A garden is an extension of a dwelling, a kind of sacred spot out of doors into which no evil thought should come and only beauty and repose find place. It has avowedly with its flowers and its seclusion an atmosphere stimulative of all the esthetic and artistic capacities. It is a spot in which to muse and to allow the finer sentiments of our nature to expand. " A garden enclosed " has been the delight of all ages and nearly all races of men. Its secluded beauty open only to heaven is an image of an ideal human soul open to upper influences but shut off in its more sacred aspects from the world. Strangely, the men of the family have not been to a great extent lovers of gardens, it would seem, in modern times, except in the period of French decadence when fops spent their time in garden flirtations. Doubtless this human depravity reacted to the detriment of the garden. Our strong and active race has not found much time for gardens. It is, however, reserved for women to get relief from the humdrum, shut-in atmosphere of the house, and doubtless many women have retained their poise and serenity through the pleasure of beautifying their gardens. It is for us Americans to redeem the garden and to make it as good a tonic spiritually as it has always been

[*Text continued on page 205.*]

ECHOES

Across majestic deeps of Echo Lake,
From wooded shores upon the silence break
Clear silver notes that make
The mountains wake
With echoes.
Against the walls with evergreen embossed,
From hill to hill the melodies are tossed
Across the peaks, and lost
Among the clouds —
Echoes of song!

They seem like memories, so sweet and clear
It startles one to find them lingering here —
The laughter, smile, and tear
Of yesteryear.
And older, fainter are the memories
That come with dying echoes on the breeze;
Their fading phantoms tease
And disappear —
Echoes of time!

Sweet songs, returning sweeter music still!
Rough notes, but discord bringing from the hill —
For busy nymphs fulfill
With good or ill
The merest thought!
What beauty fills the unseen and unheard —
The silent echoes of a thought or word,
And all the ether stirred
With vibrant life!
Echoes of thought!

MILDRED HOBBS

ACROSS ECHO LAKE—FRANCONIA

NEWPORT WATERS

esthetically.   A Chester Garden (p. 149) is an effort in one of the high
villages of New Hampshire to attain some of these desirable purposes.

The old village of Durham is now much changed and modernized owing
to its being the seat of the State Agricultural College.   Nevertheless at
least one beautiful old door remains (p. 165).   Its type reminds us
somewhat of certain Connecticut doors.   The arch in combination with
the horizontal members blends in Palladian fashion the classical Greek
with the classical Roman elements.   The small panels of the door are
a good feature.   It is seen here that the knocker is set on one side for
the sake of being based on a stile.   The window caps are of the early
type and are an excellent feature to be sought for in old dwellings.   This
style seems to have been abandoned in the latter part of the eighteenth
century.

Exeter has in the Cincinnati Chapter House (p. 173) a range of old
buildings adapted from the colonial.   It is very happy in its adaptations
and occupies a central position in the old village, doing much to dominate
its atmosphere.   There are several three story dwellings in Exeter, of the
late eighteenth century, and a few which hold over from a century earlier.
The academy at Exeter has acquired several of the early good dwellings
about the square opposite the main building and has secured thus a fine,
and what will undoubtedly be made a perpetual, feature.   The residence
of old Doctor Soule and dwellings of other worthies will, of course, be
kept as they are for future generations and will enrich and mellow and
dignify the academy environment.   We who were scholars there are to
find from generation to generation a greatly increased joy in returning to
a village containing so much of the best early American life.

The Benning Wentworth mansion at Little Harbor, Newcastle, near
Portsmouth (p. 220), has preserved some of the quaint devices on orna-
mental posts in the fences about it.   The interior (p. 289) was rather
too pretentious to be typical but is, nevertheless, of very great interest,
as being the home of New Hampshire's most famous man of that time,

[*Text continued on page* 209.]

A FAIRY HALL

There's a fairy hall in a sylvan place,
And its thousand windows are draped with lace!

The walls are enchanted, and cushioned across
With thick, rich tapestry hangings of moss!

The tables are spread with lichen and mold —
Rare treasures of emerald, copper and gold!

The wild red wood-lilies, banked with ferns,
Are scattered about in great stone urns!

And the nymphs with the dancing undines play
On a crystal floor where south winds stray!

They feast on nectar along the stream!
In the bowls of the Indian pipes they dream!

Their cobweb gowns with the dew-drop beads
Are fashioned each morn in the thimble weeds!

When the vesper sparrows are caroling songs
They flock about Jack-in-the-pulpit in throngs!

And at close of day, in the twilight glooms,
They sleep in the love vine's clustered blooms

Till the moonbeams dance in the fairy place
And the stars twinkle down through a curtain of lace!

MILDRED HOBBS

NEW HAMPSHIRE LICHEN

JUNE AMONG BIRCHES—ANTRIM

PURITY AND GRACE

who allotted some two hundred towns in New Hampshire Grants, now Vermont. His name is retained in various Wentworths and in the city of Bennington. The fireplace in the great hall is of a character sufficiently ornate to be fit for the home of a Colonial governor.

It is pleasing that this fine old property is in the hands of those who love it and will see that it is carefully cherished. The little coves and promontories of Newcastle have no small number of quaint dwellings located picturesquely. One such appears in a Newcastle Cove (p. 287). The little building in the foreground is apparently a shop connected with the old house. The ebbing and flowing of the tide gives a variety to a seaside residence like this which is necessary, perhaps, to enliven so far the monotony. Near this dwelling we noticed going to ruin a very worthy old house from which some of the doors had been wrenched. From its upper windows a fine outlook was obtainable and its location seems to us far more desirable than some others that are eagerly sought for.

The Langdon door (p. 289), one of the stately entrances of Portsmouth, is said to have been occupied, on its canopy, by Washington when he made his bow to the people of Portsmouth on his last long journey. Portsmouth was Washington's " farthest north." While here he also visited, it is said, the Tobias Lear house, where dwelt the mother of his secretary of that name. It adjoins the Wentworth-Gardner House.

We are not attempting to describe particularly the door on Pleasant Street, Portsmouth (p. 269), except to note that it is a late type and therefore shows considerable variation from those already mentioned.

Two other Portsmouth doors appear on page 113. One of them has the much to be desired twelve panels, and varies the usual bonnet top or broken arch with a broken pediment, and a lamp with a carved flame top. The other is interesting as showing the two door style, and as illustrating the somewhat late carving of ovals on the capitals and a heart on the keystone.

We would say that Portsmouth has a good half of the architectural features in the state, the others being found in Dover, Exeter and Hampton, for the most part. Of course, there are many fine dwellings dating from 1800–1840, but we make little attempt to call attention to them. Those, however, who are fond of old houses need not suppose themselves in a new country in southern or even central New Hampshire. We have here and there shown several dwellings in settings of trees or by the sides of streams to which we do not otherwise call particular attention. Almost every village in southern New Hampshire has one or more beautiful old houses, the four chimney type predominating, with its roof sloping to every side and its projecting porch.

SIGNS

A QUAINT feature of country life is found in its sign boards. There is a sign on the main road from Hillsboro to Keene (p. 57) which excited our amusement, and we have had it sketched. There were several metallic signs attached to an elm tree. As the tree grew it affectionately threw its wood about them so that in one instance only the tip of one of them shows, most of the letters of the sign being now buried in the solid wood. While they are not likely to be wrenched off by the prank of college boys they are of little value for their original purpose but as indicating a mood of nature they are most fascinating.

Along this road everything points to Keene. A farmer from whom we inquired what was hidden under the growth said with irony that whoever went on this road must go to Keene, by which he referred to the fact that there seemed to be no hints of any other towns given on the signs. The lettering done in the older pure paints sometimes stood out above the body of the sign almost like raised letters. There seems little in this country of the conventionally shaped wooden hand often seen in England, though in the vicinity of Rindge and Jaffrey such signs have been imitated presumably by some kind-hearted citizen. He shows the

A HIDDEN FOUNTAIN—WILTON

A MEREDITH ROADSIDE

SILVER STRAND—MADISON

horse galloping in the direction of the town indicated, or there are coaches or dogs which, by the way they are headed, answer the purpose of a finger or an arrow. The usual modern arrow on signs has its barb so small that it is difficult often to see, without stopping, which way it points.

There has been a great deal of worthy emulation between certain of the towns to provide good signs of late years, but most of the work still remains to be done. The signs are mostly needed not in the towns where it is easy to inquire, but in the back woods where the old house at the cross roads has burned, and the old stone post has long since lost its sign. Perhaps nothing is more exasperating to a traveler than to get into the woods a long distance from a habitation at such a corner where one road is as bad as another and there is not the slightest means of knowing what direction one should take. Possibly a remedy for this evil would be the taking up of arrangements on the part of the state to see that roads were shown, although how that could be done in relation to roads that were not subsidized by the states would remain to those who understand practical politics to work upon.

It often happens that a sign is twisted around ninety degrees from its original direction and more often that it points forty-five degrees off the true line so that one does not know which road it intends to direct us toward. This is more exasperating than not to find any sign at all.

The bureaucratic working out of colors for roads is exceedingly unsatisfactory, since such roads are now far more numerous than the seven primary colors, or any reasonable combinations of the same. One would require a year's course at a university to become thoroughly posted on the signs in New England alone, so far as they are supposed to mark state roads. It would be far more sensible to show the name of the adjoining town and below that the first important town beyond. Thus signs pointing two ways would require but four names and would mean something to the traveler if they were of uniform style. When roads get numbered up into the hundreds as they are now it is quite absurd,

[*Text continued on page* 217.]

IN MAY

Her veil is a haze of the smiling hills,
The trees are the bride's bouquet,
And blushing her way through the heavens she rides,
For Earth is a bride in May!
Her robe is a velvet of rose and white;
It sparkles with gems of dew
Where trimmings of shadow-lace stir and fall
In fluttering lines anew.

Her fragrance, the showering boughs of pink
That border the road in May,
And scatter their delicate shells of tints
Wherever the breezes stray.
And ribbons of gold are the winding roads,
Looped in bewildering maze,
To girdle with flowers the robe of Earth
And stream from her veil of haze.

O ribbons of gold are the circling roads
That lead to the peaks of snow,
And many a petal-strewn mile they wend
Where myriad blossoms grow.
The carol of birds — how wild and sweet!
And how the dull bass of bees,
And singing of winds from the far-away,
Make music among the trees!

And I know the words of the song they sing
Through the glorious bright bouquet!
They whisper the call from New Hampshire hills —
The call of the road in May!

MILDRED HOBBS

MAY SNOW FLAKES — CARROLL

SACO BIRCHES—CONWAY

AUTUMN SHADE—JACKSON

and indicates a passion for bookkeeping but not practicability. This is an age when we are in constant danger of departure from common sense, and if our road schemes run into fads and fancies in this fashion a sharp halt ought to be called to bring our customs back to normal. If one is strolling along and comes to road number 113 he may cudgel his brains in vain to know where he is. He needs a series of maps and diagrams. One other condition that every traveler has experienced is that some of the good old signs direct one by the old turnpike over the steepest hills and on roads now disused since new thoroughfares have been constructed. The old road looks inviting and in our innocence we are often led off into impracticable highways. These nuisances are so easily corrected, and often even at a saving of expense rather than at an increase of outlay, that it is to be hoped that officials will rub their eyes and wake up.

NEW HAMPSHIRE SUPERLATIVES

THERE is a valid objection to superlatives, in a too general use, partly because they become an inexact habit, and partly because they excite envy. At the expense of these dangers, however, we point out several superlatives or comparatives relating to the scenery of New Hampshire, and wait to hear from the neighborhoods not mentioned. The broadest view this side of the Rocky mountains is supposed to be had from the summit of Mount Washington. At least four states, besides Canada and the Atlantic ocean are visible in good weather. Monadnock summit is the best southern outlook.

The most beautiful lake for situation may be Chocorua. At once some will say they prefer Echo lake at Profile Notch. Our preference is based upon the finer mountain contour visible from Chocorua lake. Dublin pond would make good its claim to supremacy in the judgment of many.

The largest lake in the state and the one having most numerous bays and the greatest number of resorts about it is Winnepesaukee.

The highest lakes in the state, the sources of a long river, are those which form the fountains of the Connecticut river in the north end of the pan handle.

The highest farm in the state is said to be in Jackson, more than 2500 feet above the sea. We think it extremely doubtful that anyone has ever tallied this matter completely as it would be too great an effort.

The largest lake shared by another state is Umbagog which is rather more than half in New Hampshire, if you consider merely its western unit.

The largest body of salt water in the state is Great Bay lying west of Portsmouth, east of Newmarket and south from Dover Point. Possibly its waters may not serve as a port for fleets, but it is a solitary instance of such a body of salt water so nearly completely surrounded by land in New England.

The finest estuary in New England is probably the Piscataqua.

The most beautiful harbor we have seen on the Atlantic coast is that of Portsmouth.

The longest river in New Hampshire is the Merrimac, since the Connecticut is a boundary stream.

The worst road in New Hampshire, — but we forbear. It is an east and west route. You will find it without much search.

The finest village street in New Hampshire may be Canaan Street. Exeter has good but short streets. Chester may put in its claim, and also Haverhill and Walpole.

The best long through route, with river views, is the Merrimac valley road beginning with the state monument on the line a little south of Nashua. Its next competitor is the road from Portsmouth through Dover and Ossipee to the mountains.

The most attractive cross route may be that from Gorham to Bethlehem and Littleton.

CONWAY LIGHTS

BROODING BRANCHES—CONWAY

ST. JOHN'S CHURCH — PORTSMOUTH

BENNING WENTWORTH'S — NEWCASTLE

The most beautiful little nook in New Hampshire, of course as it impresses us, is Dixville Notch. Further, more care has been expended on the development of this site than any other similar district in the state.

The most attractive village is, perhaps, Peterboro with its beautiful public edifices, though Exeter with its academy buildings would, of course, take the precedence. Lebanon would take high rank, as would also Pittsfield.

The cleanest, most wideawake little city with attractive shops is probably Laconia.

The best rocky coast line is found at Rye.

The finest beach is at Hampton.

The oldest settlements in New Hampshire are Portsmouth and Dover, the coast line towns coming next.

The loveliest little lakeside by-road we have seen is on the margin of Ossipee.

The best general mountain view from a valley is that from Intervale or that from North Woodstock, the former of the White Mountain range proper, the latter of the Franconia Mountains.

The best place to find a quaint old house for restoration is on any road at distances of not more than five miles apart. This sentence may be execrable grammar, but it tells the truth.

The oldest house in New Hampshire may be Webster's boarding place while he was at school at Exeter, or it may be the Jackson house at Portsmouth.

The newest house in New Hampshire is not worth mentioning.

The best center of New Hampshire, from which to visit it all, is probably Concord, both because it is a pleasing city in itself and because many important roads radiate from it.

The best northern center is Bethlehem.

The greatest number of hotels at any one point is at Bethlehem.

New Hampshire is notable for its good hotels and boarding houses.

Indeed, as to the boarding house this state is perhaps the last redoubt containing any considerable number of the good old sort.

The most important centers for antique furniture are Portsmouth, Concord and Nashua. Exeter and Dover also stand well in this regard with Franklin, Keene, Claremont and Manchester among other centers. There is a shop or a dwelling where furniture, more or less early, is sold, in perhaps half of the towns in New Hampshire.

The most interesting plains district with great pine trees is found near Keene.

The most striking collections of great birch trees we have seen is on the hills of Antrim. There, near Greystone Lodge, was the monarch of them all. There are notably fine birches, however, about Dublin, the Glen, Lancaster, and almost every section that is high.

The elm roadsides of New Hampshire are notable especially in its southeastern section.

The most charming rapid river that we know is the Saco, which may be followed from Bretton Woods through Crawford Notch, Bartlett, the Conways into Fryeburg. From that point on we reserve our comments for Maine.

For quiet waters the Connecticut throughout almost its entire length on the boundary line affords compositions of beauty, exquisite and innumerable.

The smaller stream of a placid sort which has most attracted us is the Contoocook river.

Villages which are very pleasing summer centers are so numerous as to embarrass us, but without attempting a comparison here we may mention in addition to those already referred to Hillsboro, Henniker, and Hopkinton on the Contoocook; Lisbon and Littleton on the Ammonoosuc; Gorham on the Androscoggin; Bristol and Plymouth on the Pemigewasset.

Individual centers of no little interest, which have their local beauties and attractive environment, are Jaffrey, Charlestown, in the southwest; Wilton, Milford and especially Amherst in the south central portion.

A FIELD FORD—CONWAY

DOUBLE HEAD—JACKSON

WINNIPESAUKEE CLOUDS — WEIRS

FRAMED — CONWAY

WESTMORELAND CHURCH

Forest roads of great beauty are those from Chocorua to Wonalancet; and that from Woodstock north, and north of Berlin.

The intellectual center of New Hampshire, which is also a village of much beauty, is of course, Hanover. One would, perhaps, select it as the most attractive, all-the-year place of residence, with Exeter as a second and Portsmouth as a third.

Concord as the seat of the legislature and as a beautiful city in itself, with commercial possibilities, is strong in its claim on one seeking the all-around advantages of an inland, New Hampshire residence.

Aside from the mountain and lake region the most attractive county in this state is perhaps Grafton, though Hillsboro is not far behind.

The large new town of New Hampshire in the commercial sense is the lumber center of Berlin. Littleton is the northern city which has more activity than any other the season through.

The least spoiled of New Hampshire's villages are, of course, those which have not grown very much for a hundred years. These are found in the southern portion of the state, quaint little back waters of a fine civilization, very attractive in their quiet, secluded dignity and in their freedom from bustle. Hancock is such a town. Fitzwilliam and Troy are high and fine.

The mountain town desirable, perhaps above others, as a residence, is Jackson, though some would say Jefferson. We have mentioned others in connection with some special feature.

New Hampshire is peculiar among our states in this, that it has a very early civilization together with the three finest natural attractions, a seashore, a great lake and a notable mountain group. One may, therefore, dwell in New Hampshire in the midst of a mellowed district, with the architectural and social age of almost three hundred years, and yet be within reach of what men most love in natural features. At Farmington or Milton, for instance, we are within an hour of sea beaches and sea cliffs; within an hour of a great and beautiful lake; within an hour of beautiful mountain scenes and within two hours of the heart of the mountains. Those who love a fine rolling farm country would find that also all about them. This striking variety is scarcely found elsewhere except on the Pacific coast. Portsmouth is less than two hours from Boston, from Portland and from Lake Winnepesaukee. Concord is within two hours of Sunapee, of Winnepesaukee and within three hours of the White Mountains and the Connecticut river. At the same time from Concord there are trunk

MAPLE DIGNITY—CONWAY

THE POOL PATH—CONWAY

A FOLIAGE FRAME—THE GLEN

lines by rail or motor to the great southern centers. At Lakeport one may take a steamer for a sail as beautiful as any inland point affords, or he may pass over good roads to river, mountain and plain within an hour. The Conways are only about two hours from Portland and the same distance through the heart of the mountains, to the fair fields of Vermont.

AN OLD HOME ROOM

THIS is what most people want, though they often go astray in seeking to provide it. We remember that a gentleman of wealth bought a beautiful old house. The deciding factor which induced his purchase was the charm of the home room. Under the auspices of his better half this room was again furnished, but — with Victorian stuff. The result was that the room wholly lost its charm and no one went into ecstacies over it.

The room required furniture of the Revolutionary period, like simple Windsor chairs, large braided rugs, early American prints (not the Currier & Ives period), an occasional silhouette, an ancient map and, for the rest of the furniture, bandy-legged tables and a desk of the same style, with an early Windsor settee or a settle and an early American tall clock. A couple of tavern tables would have constituted all the necessary objects to add. Of course, a baby chair or two always gives a touch of interest to such a room. One or two candle stands and a sconce of a simple sort could be used. The total furnishings at the time we speak of would not have been more than two hundred or at the outside three hundred dollars. The furnishings that really were put in represented a sum two or three times that.

In such a room the fireplace is the central feature. It should always be of good size though not necessarily huge. Anything less than five feet wide is a little scant. The top should not be arched but straight, with an iron to support the brick, unless the fireplace is of stone.

A crane with a tea kettle, a small pot with its hook, a warming pan, a toaster on the hearth, an old fashioned fire shovel and tongs complete the equipment. The great danger is in adding things which are inharmonious. A single object which could not have been of the period is enough to ruin all. Even those who do not know often feel the incongruity though they cannot explain it. A little fire should always be smouldering here except during the summer heat. The heat should be supplied through radiators or registers set within the wall, so as not to obtrude their modern presence. A radiator in such a room is altogether ruinous. Besides, it is a bad thing even in a modern house so far as taste is concerned.

The ceiling of such a room need not show beams or at least anything more than a summer beam, which may be cased and painted white, if that is the wish of the owner. If the wall work is painted white or cream white or pale brown that may answer. Of course, natural pine is better. Old pine may be procured for such purposes. A room thus furnished may be very comfortable and is always charming. Wooden seated chairs may be cushioned. If one wants a chair of four or five slats in the back and a rush seat of the period say of 1720, it is not inharmonious and is very comfortable.

The errors in furnishing such a room are in the direction of elaborateness, of incongruity and of stuffiness. In the effort, generally mistaken, for elaborateness, the fireplace is furnished with a highly ornate pair of English andirons. They half spoil the room. Then one modern overstuffed chair is sneaked in, to make the room attractive for John, as the wife explains. The ruin is complete. She does not know that a rush seated chair is the most comfortable ever made, besides being durable and cleanly. How long can an overstuffed chair be used with decency? Possibly a week. Almost invariably such chairs are unclean, always unsanitary, and in bad taste. Or recent pictures, not oils, are placed on the walls. Or something is done to lose the quiet effect.

Incongruity appears in mixing various periods. Cheap modern furniture

A BOWERY FORD—CONWAY

MIDDAY AMONG MOUNTAINS—THE GLEN

MOUNTAIN MEADOWS — CONWAY

MEADOW AND MOUNTAIN — CONWAY

looks still cheaper when associated with early furniture. There is no possible excuse on the score of comfort, taste, durability or expense in using new and old together. If one insists on new furniture it should be closely copied from the old, but without an effort to pass it off for old. We have known not a few who really wished to be deceived and never turned a hand to ascertain the facts. The last error in furnishing is to crowd too much into a room. The walls particularly are rendered hideous by a large number of little sketches, run up and down in diagonals, or like the picture page of a Sunday supplement, whereas charm is secured only by a very few pictures, kept well apart. The floors are spoiled by a great assortment of little rugs. Did not Mrs. Grundy say rugs were the proper thing? So the floor is made to look like a large number of griddle cakes on a quick lunch window gas stove, only the colors of the rugs are less harmonious than the griddle cakes, and not much larger.

There must be far more open space than furniture. No, madam, your room is not arranged for a lecture, though the number of chairs would suggest it. We recall several rooms that require nothing whatever to render them charming, except to remove a few mongrel pieces of furniture. There is enough good furniture in them already. People cling to their horrible furniture almost as passionately as to their pet sins. Of course both furniture and sins are a curse to them, but who, with experience of the world, expects to find it rational?

THE BED ROOM

BED ROOMS do not give as great opportunity for going wrong, but only the slightest opening is needed to admit of large follies. Except in elegant bed rooms braided rugs will answer, though strips of rag carpet or a large rug of this material is easier to take out for cleaning.

There ought to be at least one comfortable chair for every guest, though some chambers lack that one. Particularly should white furniture be avoided. We have never been able to conceive of any occasion when white furniture was desirable. Painted furniture is often sticky, and generally in bad colors. Black or green chairs are often tolerable, but the natural light wood is best. A particular horror to be avoided is " mahoganized " furniture which is not mahogany, or mahogany in shapes in which it was never used, as in Windsor chairs. Very heavy beds are in bad taste. There are scarcely any exceptions to this statement. And of course light hangings for the beds, if any hangings are used, are always best, and the same remark applies to all draperies throughout a house. Walls should never be somber. Our dwellings are too dark. If walls must have paper the smaller the figure the better. Harmony of color scheme is everywhere important, even in a chamber.

It has been popular to use only very small tables in chambers. As a consequence the chairs are everywhere loaded with any number of articles and there is nowhere to sit. A large bed room is made very attractive by a table of good size, and of substantial structure, in addition to a stand or two. The presence of old-fashioned washstands in a modern chamber is an affectation. Neither old nor new furniture in a dwelling is good to own unless it may be used. A couch in a chamber should never be stuffed, still less overstuffed. Cane, or rush, or canvas, over which a substantial cushion is placed, is good.

THE DINING ROOM

THE sideboard, partly because the use of long bottles is no longer proper, is going out. Still, one hardly wishes to throw aside a beautiful piece of old mahogany. There may be other uses for the bottle drawers. The table to match the sideboard should have legs of the same style, whatever that is. And chairs should also harmonize in this regard. This means of course, since the sideboard belonged to the Heppelwhite and Sheraton day, that a room containing such a sideboard should be of

ALSTEAD GRACE   VISTA IN THE GLEN

THE YOUNG SACO—CRAWFORD NOTCH

FROM JACKSON HILLS

A GORGE, ISLES OF SHOALS

that period. But if one seeks the simplicity of the country style and makes the dining room suggest the ancient kitchen, a pine dresser with scrolled ends and top may go with a light refectory table and straight-legged banister-backed Dutch chairs. These chairs are uncomfortable unless they are high — at least for men. Earlier styles may use court cupboards, Carver chairs and trestle or square oak tables. A carved or decorative spoon rack is a delightful addition to a dining room. A baby's high chair of a quaint type is an essential.

If one attempts the Chippendale type in a dining room a hard task lies ahead. The sideboard table, without drawers, is, however, feasible, and Chippendale chairs, and even a pair of tables (one at least generally new to match the old)! All these pieces should be either in cabriole legs or straight legs. A smaller side table in the same style, as a serving table is good. Considerable bare spaces on the floor are best — or a plain floor. A floor of square unglazed red tiles is admirable. A fireplace helps much. Walls may be stronger in color than in any other room, and paneling is best. The ceiling also may be treated with small timbers and plaster or wood between.

We speak of a cabinet for china last of all because a good one is so difficult to find. But corner cupboards and side cupboards are admirable and with a fireplace almost make a dining room. To be sure, in the old days, the corner cupboard was more often in the parlor, but if we go back far enough we shall find that the parlor was the dining room. And when another room was reserved for dining the cupboard was left in the parlor, partly that callers might see the treasures therein.

An old tea urn, plate, fine bowls and such things may serve to finish the dining room. But never should we forget to harmonize the periods. Pine and mahogany do not agree. Maple and pine go very well together. Wall clocks, in spite of the dictum of etiquette, are good in dining rooms. But in what old house do we find plate rails?

A LITTLE MOUNTAIN LAKE — JACKSON

MOWING AMONG MOUNTAINS

BEYOND THE FIELD WALL — LACONIA

ELEMENTS OF OUTDOOR BEAUTY

THE principal features composing outdoor attractions are water, sky, hills and foliage. The water scenes divide into marine, lake and stream subjects. Between the differences provided by the seasons, by the varying light of morning, noon and night, and by the shadings of color and the changing shapes, we should say, perhaps, that the sky is more interesting than the earth itself.

The hills or mountains afford two totally different effects, depending on the fact whether they are near or afar. When near at hand the cultivated slope or tree-decorated hillocks have an appeal and an aspect that is quite foreign to the distant blue or purple masses of mountains.

Under foliage we may class, for pictorial uses, everything that grows, but the chief division is between gardens and trees. In any landscape, not a marine, trees are, whatever the background may be, the principal feature, whether they are felt to be so or not, by the beholder. The variety of shapes, in the curvature of the limbs of trees, is a perennial charm, since it partakes of every line of beauty that is conceivable. Some trees, like the gray birch, growing in clusters, will after a storm present the shape of a perfect bow, rising from the earth and sweeping back to the earth again, in bended masses weighted down by snow. Again, in the elm shapes, we get an effect almost similar to what is called the weeping elm, which sometimes by the water side, or even on lawns, sweeps in an ox-bow shape from the trunk upward, outward, and downward again, until it trails in the water or brushes the turf. The growth of the oak is quite different in every feature. It lacks regularity in the contour of its branches, and, curiously enough, this irregularity is perhaps the largest element in its charm. It would be impossible to imagine the strength and contour of an oak limb unless one had seen it darting back and forth and upward and downward. However induced, this shape seems to impart a suggestion of power and of conflict, of victory and

THE FIRST HOUSE, DANIEL WEBSTER ROAD

of ruggedness. One gets the feeling that it has withstood so much that nothing will overthrow it.

The ash tree inclines to be somewhat scraggly, and is decidedly lacking in grace as compared with other trees in our climate. At its best it is passable. The willow, somehow, while seen now and then in paintings, never appeals to the public. The public speak in admiration of it, but they never desire to see it in paintings, at least where it is the dominating feature. It presents a sameness of outline and a lack of any special symmetry or feature of admiration, as compared with other species of trees.

The maple has perhaps its greatest charm in its general outline as a unit viewed from afar. It assumes the form of a true ball or of a cone, more or less pointed, in the sugar loaf form. Where it is unhindered in its growth it almost invariably, when it escapes the disaster of storms, takes on naturally an almost perfectly circular form, at the extremity of its branches. Its branches, therefore, must be considered not separately, but as a part of the whole tree, in producing artistic effects. In the changing of its color in the autumn it often happens that the

MT. WASHINGTON

CONWAY MEADOWS

LOW WATER—CONWAY

A CHARMING OLD AGE—CONWAY

tree becomes parti-colored, and thus appeals to us in two aspects. Perhaps one side will be red and the other side yellow. Again, the leaves may assume a uniform coloring, or they may be mottled or veined or edged with various combinations, so that the maple leaf is the first form of beauty, perhaps, that appeals to a child. It first seems to awaken the sense of harmony and contrast and form in an awakening mind, as the boys and girls wade through the masses of leaves, and toss them in their play. Fifty years ago it was the recognized thing in the country to preserve and varnish maple leaves, and arrange them under glass or in books. We should be free from any disrespect for this childlike awakening to art, because anything that will open the heart of a child to the appreciation of beauty is a very distinct step in good education.

Another tree which here and there decorates our eastern landscapes is the individual cedar of the small sort. It grows in pastures and waste lands or by fence rows, usually in a pointed compact form, which contrasts in beauty with the round maple or the curving elm. It constitutes the best of features in a New England landscape.

The majestic and dependable tree for the year around is of course the pine, which in its finest development is most satisfactory in its comforting power, shielding us as it does from the storms of winter and the suns of summer. We have, perhaps, in these latter days too much neglected the evergreens. Particularly on our roadsides we have planted the more ephemeral trees, like the maple, which are easily subject to injury of the bark, and are, perhaps, the last trees that should be planted by the roadside. The pine is admirably fitted for those considerable districts of New England where the soil is very light. Indeed, all over the east, there are streaks of fat and lean soil, as it were, like a slice of bacon. It is in these lighter soils that evergreens naturally do well. By fostering evergreen growths in such soils a great part of the more dreary tracts throughout our whole country, where trees grow, are to be more and more a resource of beauty and protection and of wealth.

The spruce gives us a conical outline quite different in form from that of the maple and affords a very symmetrical shape, and gives a note of color that differentiates it from the pine, and, indeed, from all other evergreens. This is especially true of the Norway spruce, with its bluish tint. It affords a very decisive punctuation in a landscape, and gives a totally different aspect to grounds from that afforded by other growths. Happily, it is being a great deal cultivated, in these days, and already forms a very striking and beautiful note by the sides of our drives.

The hemlock, more or less despised in the past, commercially, nevertheless has its place, as it is humbly willing to spread its graceful branches anywhere, and to fill in niches otherwise unoccupied. The hemlock branch, with the old and new growth, is one of the most exquisite things in nature. It is only its commonness that has led us to pass it by. Its effect, either minutely viewed, or in a general view, is most fascinating.

The beech, in its ordinary light bark, or in its specialty as the copper beech, is an object of great interest, wherever found. It invariably indicates fine soil where it grows naturally, in any abundance, and is a safer criterion in selling lands than the word of the most honest real estate agent. In this respect it is superior even to the rock maple. A beech tree, in its manifold ramifications, affords a sense of exuberance and wealth to one who wanders in a forest of this species. We cannot imagine any finer exhibition in the natural world of great abundance, and joy of nature, than such a forest.

Among the fruit trees the pear tends to height and narrowness when left to develop naturally, and suggests vertical panels. The apple on the other hand with its broad spread, and somewhat oak-like habit of limb, suggests horizontal panels. In its extensive habitat, whether wild or cultivated, with its blossoms filling the valley and running over the hills, edging into the woodlands, and glowing from every odd corner, it absolutely dominates an eastern landscape in the spring. That is as true in Maryland as in New Hampshire, perhaps more so. The Maryland orchards are wonderful. The sentiment connected with the apple blossom, as the quite obvious decoration for weddings, has perhaps in-

A QUIET DAY—LACONIA

ALBANY WATERS

THROUGH THE STREAM—MILTON

HALL OF PIERCE HOUSE, PORTSMOUTH

creased the degree of attention paid to it. But its natural beauty surpasses that of the rose, perhaps, in its finest estate. Apple blossoms considered as a collection of clusters, in the delicacy of their shading, from its earliest bud-reds to pearl white, are not possible to surpass in charm. This beauty is greatly enhanced by the irregularity of the small branches, in combination with the perfection of the flowers. This feature, by its great contrast, makes the flowers more beautiful.

It is quite amazing how different kinds of trees, at different periods of the seasons, dominate the landscape. Quite early the birches spread over the hillsides, in certain regions, so that one would say they were the only sort of tree growing in the vicinity. In other districts the red or swamp or water or soft maple, variously so called, may fill the valleys to the apparent exclusion of all other foliage.   Later on it appears that the whole country is one mass of apple blossoms, which call attention away from every other sort of growth, and make one feel that the spring belongs to the apple tree.   In the autumn again the strength of the maple coloring takes possession of whole townships, so that we can scarcely think of any other tree.   This aspect of the seasons is most important in increasing our enjoyment of outdoor life, so much so that a country which is about equally decorated with these varieties of trees has a sequence of beauty that imparts a different phase of scenery to the same outlook.

Again, when winter comes, some landscapes seem to be all evergreens, as of course they are the only trees that give any mass of color at that season, though in certain sections the scrub oak will tenaciously exhibit its foliage the winter through.   One sees at once the obvious advantage of mingling these strong dominant features in any landscape, so that it may never be without its charm, and may ever contribute a new note to the season, and remind us that life is a succession of revelations in beauty and in strength.

At times when the snows have a clinging softness the entire landscape may again be a frost world, whose beauty cannot be rivaled even by the spring or summer glories.   Ice storms have a sinister beauty, like that of two years ago, when such masses clung to the trees that there was a general wreckage that will not be overcome fully in a generation.   Nevertheless as the sun glinted upon this world of encysted branches, the grandeur was startling, and never to be forgotten.   It would appear that the play of the seasons, and of the rain and sun and wind on foliage, altogether afford the greatest charm of outdoor living.   For this beauty is always in evidence, and even when, as often happens, the sky is more or less tame, the zenith being a faded, whitish blue, the foliage, or the ramifications of the trees, always afford us objects of admiration.   More and more the wonder of tree growth impresses us as we study it.

Trees are the greatest natural historical monument, in this respect perhaps surpassing rocks.   Rocks may give data of an earlier period but

WASHINGTON CLOUDS

MADISON WATERS

SILVER LAKE — MADISON

A SECLUDED ROAD — JACKSON

they remind us of the glacial age. When we remember how the ancient tree growth is being brought back to us in the coal measures and in the dyes now extracted from coal tar, we may rejoice in the fact that primeval landscapes did not display themselves in vain. For ages to come the world will be beautiful by the resurrection of these colors. It is every bit of it preserved in the deep-hid coal mines, and all that we want of it is available for all time. Therefore, the present tree growth is simply a continuance of the blazonry of joy and glory which has spread over the valleys and raced up the mountains from time immemorial. The trees also, in their marvelous growth bands, tell their age with a certainty that cannot be rivaled by any of our human records, and they even indicate the recurrence on certain years of forest fires which they have survived, an illustration recently being given of a tree that had suffered many fires and survived them all.

Any species of our trees is a monument of vitality and helpfulness, when we consider the terrible ravages of the insect world, concerning which some have feared that they would overwhelm civilization, and perhaps all life.

When we see a magnified insect we get a picture surpassing in monstrosity and voracity and apparent lack of morals any possible conception of an evil spirit, as described by a Dante or a Milton. A magnified house fly, mosquito or locust, is as horrible as any nightmare seen by a victim of delirium tremens. It is, therefore, a kind Providence that created them small, because if they were large they would render life a horror to be avoided. When we see that the fair beauty and strength of the trees has survived all these attacks and that it has existed in glory, and majesty, and a sense of triumph, we are encouraged to believe that the beneficent power inherent in evolution has not lost its hold. In fact, the only objection that any impatient man could raise to evolution, in these days, is that there is not enough of it. So far as the anthropoid man is concerned, we feel that we want to hasten this evolution. The same is true in relation to trees. We wish to do what we can to enhance their glory and maintain their permanent strength. We do not know whether at some epochs of the earth the majesty of the sequoia gigantea extended over vast areas of surface, but we see in the narrow range that it now occupies forces evidently at work to kill out gigantic trees, just as, with the exception of the whale, the forces at work in animal forms seem to work against size. Nevertheless, we cannot think that this gigantic cousin of the redwood is a monster, in any sense that is unpleasant. Evidently it is a tree that will not do well in a very rainy or a very cold climate. We do not know whether efforts to propagate it are meeting with any fair degree of success, and we do not know that such efforts should succeed, since we have the oak.

THE OAK IN OUR HUMAN HISTORY

THE oak is absolutely the tree on which we should expend our efforts if we love the connection of strength and beauty sufficiently to seek to make it a dominating feature in our landscapes. The oak will flourish under a great variety of conditions and from year to year afford great comfort and joy, feeding the esthetic sense as well as our longing for permanence. It will abide with us through a sufficient number of generations, so that one may find that the possession, on a home estate, of several fine oaks, ties together a family line in a more perfect way than any other possible human feature. It has been reckoned that the three hundred years of American history which now extend to eleven generations, as some generations run, if doubled by a similar period of three hundred years of English history, lead back every human being of English descent in America to a number of ancestors equal to the population of England six hundred years ago. That is to say, potentially, we are, some of us, related to all the people who existed in England in the thirteenth century. Of course, actually, there was less moving about, at that time, of the peoples, than in the eleventh century, and in various other periods of English

NEW HAMPSHIRE.—INTERVALE

A FORD AT THE MAPLE

A CONWAY CRAG—ECHO LAKE

history. Nevertheless, the oak tree in some instances, even in America, had attained its full majesty, and had perhaps passed its meridian, in the case of some examples still existent, six hundred years ago. In this aspect, therefore, we find that a family may tie itself to the oak tree in the sections where our race should exist successfully and is still maintaining itself. The oak tree must be more and more upon our thought as the proper species to cultivate about home grounds, and by the side of a stone edifice protected by modern methods from dampness, so as to be conducive to health, and erected with strength to rival the continuance of the oak. We look forward to the time when the natural love for family tradition, and a proper pride in the achievements of our ancestors, will make it a general object among intelligent American families to create such a homestead, thus protected by the oak. This tree may connect all the phases of history that are now lost to us, and may record the years through which our families have tied themselves up, in a degree, with all humanity. In

THE PIERCE HOUSE FIREPLACE

relation to these ramifications of heredity we may think of the oak tree as in a sense a family tree.

The immigrant to America was of a mixed race. The first main strain that we recognize in this race was the Kelt as found in Britain. The Roman occupation, of some four hundred years, certainly gave to our race some tincture of Roman blood. The inroad of the Saxon peoples mingled with this new strain. The Saxons themselves undoubtedly had some touch of the Tartar. The new race resultant was later mingled with the Danes, and last of all with the Norman blood. The modern American of English stock, therefore, while perhaps mainly Keltish or Saxon, has a greater or less mixture of at least three other human families. This modern American is also related by blood with the kings, heroes, sages and scoundrels of six hundred years ago. Good and bad, whatever we are, we have lived under the oaks for six hundred years, and we might have lived under the same oak while all these changes took place, finding it, at the beginning of our career, of majestic size, and still seeing it hale and hearty. Our pride of family and of human achievement may be humbled when we are reminded of the persistent quiet strength of a single specimen of a certain species of tree. It is to the writer a fascinating chain of thought, and not the less so because somewhat fanciful and possibly misty, that we may connect ourselves more fully with the personality of trees. When, in an Eastern landscape, we have a collection of fine individual oak trees about a dwelling, and near by a fair stream, a slope and a meadow, and, behind, a fine majestic hillside, rising perchance to the dignity of a mountain; and where, dug from the earth, we have fine materials for a permanent dwelling, and for solid and substantial walls, we have an assemblage of elements of beauty, of strength, of history, and of imagination, which combined are very satisfactory to the mind. Those periods in the human life when we are not definitely devoted to some certain object are perhaps longer in their total duration than are the hours engaged in special occupations. The morning, the evening, the noon hour, the waking hours of the night, and

AN ECHO LAKE DOME

THE UPLIFT OF THE HILLS — JACKSON

A POOL — LACONIA

A FARM AT THE FORD — BEMIS

many an interval in our working hours, when pausing to look up from the hoe, or gazing up as we go to our work, in the orchard, we may feed our minds on this sense of beauty and permanence interwoven in the history of tree growth in a landscape, with the culture features carried out by our ancestors. We ourselves are a part of the landscape. Most of us came from the sod and most of us, considered at least in the standard of avoirdupois, go back to the sod. That inscrutable and indefinable something which is called the soul, and which some people, more fanciful even than the writer, allege has been photographed, and which still others have testified has weight, and tips the scales at one half ounce or thereabouts, this inscrutable force is the connecting and dominating link which ties together all natural phenomena, whether they are changing or permanent.

We were recently reading again the admirable *Life of Washington* by Washington Irving. We find in Washington so large a degree of common sense that when accused by the English of being merely a country squire, he himself joyed in the thought, and was the last person to wish to deny the accusation. He considered himself by no means lost out from the importance of history when he was cultivating his acres, which he loved far more than the power of command over men. He loved tree planting. He loved turning up the richly colored sod. He walked his bounds with the greatest satisfaction, and joyed in that original and eternal source of wealth, namely, what arises from the brown earth. He looked on his river through the foliage, and over the turf, and was content. Was he, therefore, a small man? We do not hear more than a whisper in his life about his ancestors. He was too busy in the present, whether in public or private duties, to dwell largely on the past. But he planted his trees. Today the most valuable monument of Washington is found in the estate that he developed and dwelt on. It is true indeed that the ideas which he advocated and embodied in the Constitution; it is true indeed that the character which was exhibited in all his acts, were all of vast importance to us, but we make the point that these things are enshrined about the dwelling and the grounds, where he labored and thought. It is fitting that his tomb also should be on his own grounds, which he loved!

The connection of human personality with trees is a subject which will bear a very large magnification in the future of our race. Here and there throughout the country we are nursing young trees that were planted by notable persons. We have all, of course, mourned over the final extinction of the elm at Cambridge under which Washington took command of the American army, and, perhaps still more than that, we lament the passing of the Charter Oak in Hartford. Nevertheless, in the process of the ages, if enough time and care is given to this subject, we may tie the history of a man to a tree, that may live after him for a thousand years.

The finest oaks in America are almost equal in size and beauty to the oaks of England. But our oaks have not, with the exception of the Charter Oak, very largely served as historical or sentimental landmarks. In a land like Palestine where fine trees were rather rare, oaks marked the dwelling places of great personages. Sublimity is imparted to any landscape blessed with here and there a majestic tree. The sense of individuality is strongly accentuated by being connected with a strongly marked landscape, where distinguished groupings of great trees are made use of to combine in the entire setting of a dwelling and its attendant structures. The surname Oakes serves to indicate the connection of the first Oakes with a residence marked by that tree.

SURNAMES AND NATURAL FEATURES

THE naming of men from their residences became a mark of aristocracy because solid men clung to the same lands. We have many families named from trees beginning with Forest (or with a doubled r) itself. There are also Woods, Woodward and Tree. We have

THE TIPS OF THE MOUNTAINS — MADISON

THE MEADOW STREAM — OSSIPEE

JACKSON HOLLYHOCKS

MOUNTAIN WATERS

families named Birch, Ashe, Beech and Larcher, which last named is a commercial partner with Mr. Branch. Even Bush is not as humble as it sounds.

THE FARM NAMES

IF WE get us a farm and wish assistance in putting it in order, we may find Messrs. Apple, Appleman and Appleyard, two of these met within a week past. Plum and Plumb, while they might dispute, between an ancestry of orchardists and lead miners, will come to our assistance if we can afford them. But Plummer is obvious. We are not acquainted with Pear, but Pearmain we know. Mr. Peach was a boyhood chum, and Mr. Lemon was the proprietor of the Wayside Inn. If we wish to enclose a field we may find a Mr. Wall, and even Stones. It is a Wells who will get water for us, unless we have Fontaine, or Spring. We have our Brooks, Rivers and even a Lake. Messrs. Waters and Drinkwater are with us. But Sir Cloudsley Shovel disdains the instrument after which he was named and has taken to the sea. For the general divisions of our farm we shall have Mr. Field, or Fifield (Fivefield) who was one of the writer's grandfathers. Messrs. Lea and Downs, Meadows, Fell, Hill, Vail, Lane, Moore, Fenn, may, each for himself take charge of the section of the farm which naturally belongs to him. We shall even have our Mudd, and a gentleman of that name in the South who was a great admirer of the statesman, christened his son Clay. Mr. Sand and Mr. Mead will be found. In our garden we shall have a Gardiner, and even a Turnipseed (one of our subscribers). Mr. Berry will be there, followed hard by Berryman. Mr. Hoe, however, has forsaken us to make printing presses, though Coward (Cowherd) and Shepherd may stick to their jobs. Ploughman and Husbandman come at our call. Mr. Plant will put in the seed, Mr. Oates and Mr. Wheat will grow, and Mr. Thresher will do his work. Then there is Mr. Farmer himself, and Woodman and Woodmansee. Senator Pepper will accompany Mr. Bean, and Mr. Sage will stand by Mr. Pease. But Mr. Weed is the most prominent gentleman present. When we go abroad into field or orchard Messrs. Budd and Blossom will be there before us, Heard or Hurd will drive up the cows, Pitcher will help with Hay and Hayes; while the landscape and the sky will give us Messrs. Redd, Brown, Dunn, Greene and Gray, Black and White, and some others, probably.

Should we wish, as who does not, to restore the old farmhouse, we shall have to assist us, if we can pay them, a Sill and a Sleeper, a Post and a Rafter, while Boardman and Naylor (old spelling of Nailer) will carry on their work, and Sawyer, Turner, Carpenter, Smith, Locke, Mason and Slater will finish it. The interior will be looked after by a lordly Stair, a Hall, Chambers and Garret. Painter will brighten it, and Glass show an amusing mirror of society, assisted by Paine. Our House will do, for that is the builder's name, and Mr. Shedd helped him. We have nearly done. After circling the Dale with our friend Walker, seeing the Flowers, and resting on Banks, — Fairbanks at that, — we pass through the pasture, and, avoiding Mr. Horn, and Mr. Bull, we reach the Gates, having made the Rounds.

A VACATION IN THE COUNTRY

ALL desire such a vacation, and all can afford it.

The first error of the vacationist is his endeavor to carry the city with him into the country, and to tell the country man how things are done in town. But those who turn their faces toward the country should first of all forget all that is behind them, because only thus will their minds freshen, and only thus will they have full attention to learn the wonders of hill and dale. How many go back to the city without any knowledge of the trees which sheltered them or the grasses through which they waded! They sat on rocks marked by glacial lines, or wrinkled by pressure and heeded it not. They failed to mark the effects of erosion or alluvial deposit; they did not attend on the mysteries of the graft, and thus lost a fascinating phenomenon.

AWAY FOR THE WHITE HILLS!—THE GLEN

THE GATE BY THE FORD

A CORNER OF WINNIPESAUKEE

ARCH WITHIN ARCH, PORTSMOUTH

Whoever goes away from the country without being enriched has not been responsive to the calls about him. The mysteries and joys of bird life are abundant delight for more than one summer. The observation of bees has occupied and delighted the most astute minds. The glory of the flowers, the varieties of forest growths, and so many other channels of interest are open to us that it is difficult for the farmer to conceal his contempt for his city visitor who becomes bored by the country.

Excursions for picking berries on the hills are delightful, for the old pastures passed through, the viewpoints gained, the fresh upland winds, the luncheon under the pines, and the return, in the afternoon light, carrying some token in our fruit baskets that we have made use of our fun.

A day passed in hunting forest mosses and lichen and ferns is sure to be joyous. A day with a small camera, carefully used with a tripod, is perhaps best of all. Why not seek out the little details in the corners of the woodland, and prove that we have had our eyes well open? The grasses are among the most beautiful of all growths, especially when in summer flower. If one is doubtful about the witch stick, sport is made by a trial with the easily available hazel fork. The gathering of flags for cat-tails or for rush seats with a trial at using the twisted strands is not without interest.

The selection of sites for dwellings may fill with great pleasure many a summer day. This is a game of solitaire, or it may be played with any number of partners. Each is to give the salient reasons for his choice of a site: the outlook, the drainage, the proximity of building materials. Each is to show how the trees about his site will lend themselves to decorate the homestead and where the paths are to wind. Then we must justify the orienting of the dwelling and the location of the outbuildings. We are to show how an old lane, or a new one, will afford a good approach, and how a little arch over a brook may give character to the house drive. We are to notice what protection there is on the north, and perhaps the west, and how the site will appear on approaching it, and how the element of surprise is to be availed of in the drive or the paths. We must settle on

WASHINGTON ACROSS A POOL

GRANT'S POND

MT. WASHINGTON AHEAD!—PINKHAM NOTCH

possible sources of water supply, and we must locate the flower, the vege-
table and the small fruit gardens. In these days we require to consider
freedom from noise and dust. Such planning is enough to satisfy keen
minds and is not too abstruse for the average mind.

No small pleasure may be had in scheming the improvement of the
dwelling which is our temporary home. When that is done we have
the matter of its surroundings to better.

In the forests we may try the game of naming the possible and profitable
uses of the various species of trees — their nuts, their bark and their wood.
We may hunt the burls which grow on the oaks or maples; we may lay
out paths to the hill crests and erect seats of loose flat rocks, or construct
nooks to shelter one from the wind.

We are not forgetting fishing, but we leave it as a subject too obvious,
and already well considered by many writers. The same is true of
hunting.

But the New Hampshire sport of " guessing," that is, estimating or
forming a judgment, is an excellent exercise for the mind. It covers
everything from the weight of a hog to the age of a woman. To " guess "
how many tons of hay a field will produce, how many potatoes there will
be to the acre, or how fast a horse will go in a race are all the basis of
business and sport. The vacationist may derive amusement by pitting
his wit against the farmer's as to the length of barns, the height of the
thermometer, the question of weather or what Sarah will have for dinner.
One uncle of ours would never turn about without asking the boy to
" guess." It was good training for judgment, and one of the best possible
practical drills in education. It is astonishing to note how a good judge
will tell to an inch the girth of an ox. The farmer deals very much in
matters that require a training in making up one's mind from partial data.
At this game he usually wins.

The naming of the animals on a farm is no end of amusement. Some
of them may have names but the visitor may go on with his new arrange-
ment. To find an appropriate name for the reliable old speckled hen,

or the gay young pullet, to learn to distinguish the sheep, and especially
to designate the cows, takes nice weighing of reasons. This last occupation the writer used to indulge in while seeking slumber. The first four
cows came easily, — Daisy, Daffodil, Buttercup and Clover. The next
quartet were slower in formation, — Meadowsweet, Heather, and — but a
somewhat weary voice is heard from the other side of the bed: " Oh, call
her Thoroughwort, and turn over and go to sleep! "

HOW TO SPEND MONEY

WE MEAN, of course, in the country. And we mean it profoundly.
If anything is capable of rousing a normally decent person to high
fever and the verge of profanity it is the manner of spending money in the
country. One would hardly conceive it possible to expend a half million
on a country place and secure no charm, no allurement, no dignity, no
serenity and no permanence. But this impossible thing has been done, is
being done and will be done, till the spendthrifts cease from muddling, and
profaners are at rest. Wilful persons continue to throw out the challenge,
" have we not the right to spend our money according to our own
notion? " As well may a South Sea Islander covered with brass ornaments
and wearing a huge ring in his nose ask the same question. We have a
legal right to do many things that no decent man will do. The Pharisee
was within his legal rights when he passed the — crippled motorist by
the roadside.

The exercise of legal rights sometimes does, and oftener ought to put a
stigma on the person who flaunts such rights. He cannot exercise, perhaps,
those legal rights, without transgressing every moral, social and esthetic
right. We have in mind a person who painted his buildings in blue and
yellow stripes and lettered huge and offensive signs upon other parts of
his buildings, in spite against his neighborhood. The law passed by the
legislature could not touch him, but he was condemned under every other

THE BRIDGE ARCH—CORNISH

A MOUNTAIN CURVE—JACKSON

THE RUSSET WOODLAND—WATERLOO

THE OLD PARSONAGE, WESTMORELAND

law known to society. In somewhat, though possibly less degree, one who expends money to mar a country landscape sins against those laws which are implanted eternally in human minds. It does not help the case a little bit that the spendthrift thinks he is doing God service, because as long as he so thinks he will not reform.

The right of beauty to a place in our thoughts, our creations and our landscapes is an indefeasible right. No practise, no ignorance to the contrary can excuse a sin against beauty.

The man who thwarts the development of beauty, or who in any manner contributes to the over abundant ugliness in the world is like one who would put out one of the stars, or establish some horror in the heavens for the world to shudder at. That the transgressor knows better, means, put in another form, that he hates knowledge and is not seeking after the pure, the beautiful, and the good. The right to be charming denied to a landscape by some wretched work upon it is analogous to planting an unsightly wart upon the face of beauty. Whoever tries to justify himself for such conduct deserves no more respect than the boy who won't go to school, but remains wilfully ignorant.

Considered broadly there is sufficient wealth in America to make all our country attractive in a few years. But undirected, wilful wealth can never accomplish any good in town or country. It is at least a hundred times as easy to make money as to spend it properly.

What law, human or divine, can be cited to justify the erection of an imitation in wood of a French chateau? Yet how many hundred thousand such dwellings make nightmares of our streets and country landscapes! And architects were accessory before the fact, because forsooth their clients *wanted* such things! What a revolution to righteousness would occur if we ceased to give men what they want, but instead gave them something a great deal better!

The travesty of art, the degradation of morals, the low plane of public taste, the waste of substance by billions, and in short the failure of civilization to rise and become grand, is all traceable to this pandering by men who know better to other men who have the dollars. The worst feature in the whole matter is that the intelligence and taste of the country is the chief sinner. It knows better than it does. It sells itself. It builds what is not worth building, manufactures hideous mongrel things because they " sell."

If there was a higher degree of morality among educated people there would be more beauty in the world. There would be a lifting to better levels instead of a dropping, as at present, to the lowest level. Art and beauty will never come to their own until they are counted more important than bread. Then indeed it will be worth while to be alive.

The hideous and soon useless bridges of steel will be replaced by perma-

DENMAN THOMPSON'S DRIVE — SWANSEA

A SCHOOLHOUSE ROMANCE — WESTMORELAND

A NEWINGTON COVE

CLOUDS ALL! — LEBANON

nent arches of beauty. The roadside poles will be banished. The desecration of trees will cease. Flimsiness will give way to graceful strength. Natural beauty will not be banished to make way for formal grounds. The interior desecrater will be banished to some far isle where he may use his bizarre horrors on the walls of wigwams. The colors of buildings will not stand out like rouge on an otherwise good face. Men who spend will better the country rather than gash it and stripe it.

Convention is a god who fights against improvement. If you want a proper molding for your doors you are told that is not a " stock " molding, that it must be made specially. In Greece the stock molding was the best, not the worst. You are met on all sides by bad customs, which require heroism, patience and a fine purposeful ideal to overcome.

The writer was recently invited to see a room corner named after him and done by a designer. The only possible decent feature in this corner was the window drapery! The furniture was of three kinds, all undefinable, all bad. The walls were bad, the floor was bad, and the ceiling was stamped steel of a design used in bars and nickleodeons! The owner proudly dragged the writer in to see a signal " room corner " done in the writer's honor! And the rest of the room did not even avow itself to be like the corner! The first element in taste would seem to demand that at least everything within the four walls of a room should be harmonious, even if, as is too often the case, one steps through the door into another " period." New Hampshire can make good her claim to fair treatment. She herself is most fair.

But where, in New Hampshire, or elsewhere for that matter can one go to an inn winning in all its dominant features, and also safe? Where, in any state, has there been a successful effort to render natural beauty more beautiful and available? On a certain famous mountain road, not in New Hampshire, motors *cannot stop* without transgressing regulations, and there is no parking spot! Here was a million spent on a very short section, to allow the public an outlook. There was a natural platform for a view, but, it being over a fence, the lover of beauty was liable to arrest if he set foot on it, though it belonged to the state! Also it is forbidden to make pictures on this road, because the state hopes to make a profit from its hack photographs!

The laws, customs, habits, business of the land, all seem inimical to the enhancement of beauty. There are millions for monstrosities but scarce a cent for charm. This is not because no effort is made to decorate. But the effort is mostly analogous to the inch-thick, shored-up, false fronts of village shops, east and west. It is not that Americans are mean. They are the most generous people on earth. But they spend their fortunes for shams, for things that ring false to truth in art. New Hampshire being first in summer visitors — at least at one time, became first in that distressful creation, the barrack of tinder called a summer hotel. How many fireproof hotels are there in New Hampshire? Can one not count on one's fingers all the fine private estates that are at once beautiful and substantial? Ugliness is still the rule. Many pretentious places have, and many more will, when their owners die, lapse into early ruin, and prove not only practically complete losses but will be monuments of ridicule, and will deprive the world of what might have been, at the same expenditure, an endless source of pleasure and permanent enrichment of country life, in dignity and charm.

Every one on a first attempt, is likely to make a mistake, if his undertaking requires a combination of efforts. But when one builds in the country one builds for a lifetime, and any error is perpetuated until such a time as fire or decay wipes out the scars on nature's breast. Therefore it is of utmost importance that those who build should first see what all students count as the best in the particular line to be attempted. It is fatal to make a serious error because such an error is too expensively corrected.

Harmony with the surroundings, a sense of solidity, a fine site, agreement with long proved good taste, absence of decoration except in classical material, — these five necessary things are easily secured in New Hampshire. If not secured the fault will not lie in the absence of opportunity.

KEENE WATERS

THE CANOE STRAND — SPOFFORD LAKE

PORTSMOUTH FROM SOUTH ST. BRIDGE

CONCORD GRASSES

HANOVER GREEN

OPEN AIR AND SANITY

IF WE should maintain a statement as startling as this, that out-of-door life is necessary to sanity, we presume our own sanity might be questioned. Yet something almost as strong can probably be proved. The office man and the student lose their sense of perspective if they confine their labors too much. Milton was a dreadful pedant and his work smells offensively of the midnight oil. Only his transcendent genius and his garden, wherein he is supposed to have dictated at least occasionally, has saved his work. What would a man who roamed the hills and strode by the streams of England have wanted of all the vast mass of Milton's recondite references to classical tales and his list of names, caught in a drag net, which passed through all known records?

The country woman, as has been said, often suffers from insanity, but her husband, who lives out of doors, shows far less tendency to a diseased mind. Italian women who seem to hate four walls are as sane as their husbands.

That occasional temporary insanity such as appeared in the greenback craze in Maine and in populism in Kansas is, after all, only a phase that quickly passes. We would be far from maintaining that out-of-door life alone can create a sage. We only say that education coupled with an out-of-door life produces a mind of fine balance.

It might be said with a show of probability that automobiles would better the American citizen by taking him out of doors. With the tendency, however, to closed cars, which are now in quite general demand, it may be questioned whether one may not as well remain at home as to get into a nearly air tight box and begin to smoke. Indeed, there is danger under these circumstances that the American will degenerate into a rather poor sort of jerked meat.

Under these circumstances what is a man to do? He dares no longer tramp on our roads, even our remote country roads. If he stops for a rest he may be transported to eternity, not by angels but by a four wheeled monster. There would seem to be only one resort, i.e., to buy country acres and wander over them. There the worst danger from beneath will be poison ivy and devil's lice, while from above the dropping of an airplane on one is still, happily, a remote possibility.

Such races as the Hebrews, who have for many generations been hived together, show indeed in many instances an abnormal keenness of mind. But it is abnormal though keen. That is to say it lacks the healthy balance that comes to one through living in the open air, where our remote ancestors spent nearly all their time. It is conceivable that in the process of aeons the human race may learn to thrive in a continuously hived life, but at present and for many generations we shall reach rotundity only by living to some degree as our fathers have lived, as regards eating and exercise. The human frame will bear an amazing amount of abuse. It is, however, not altogether a misfortune that as a rule it is only three generations from shirt sleeves to shirt sleeves. If people will not live rationally they cannot keep up an abnormally high rate of specialized brain production. Indeed, it is a question whether any brain can work at its highest effi-

A NEWCASTLE COVE

A NEWCASTLE REACH

HANOVER CLOUDS

A HANOVER BEND — CONNECTICUT RIVER

LANGDON DOOR
PORTSMOUTH

BENNING WENTWORTH'S
NEWCASTLE

ciency day in and day out for more than two hours a day. Some would limit the time to one hour a day. At least, a brightness and breadth of thought is likely to be lost by steady application. So much is this the truth that it may without exaggeration be stated that the more time we spend on certain pieces of work, the poorer is that work. We may dash off, when we are at the top of condition, something really good that the world will want, whereas were we to delve on such an effort for twelve hours a day we should prove uniformly humdrum.

The out-of-door life brings sanity partly because a pressure of gas induced by an indoor life on organs like the hearts and the lungs prevents the normal flow of oxygen through the blood and the brain becomes morbid. Heavy eating and light exercise has killed more genius than has ever been manifested in the world.

Nor let any man suppose that this out-of-door life need be undertaken as a means of exercise. Whoever comes to it in that spirit, so lacking in discernment, will not derive much benefit from it. He who strolls over his pasture at the edge of the woods and fails to see the chipmunks and to notice the birds' nests and to see the wild flowers by the stone-wall may, indeed, almost as well remain indoors, because if he is fretting over his exercise the reaction will neutralize the benefit of it.

It has been proved that fear and unpleasant excitement generate poison in the blood. It appears, therefore, that he who does not love the country should learn to love it. It is the love of it that will lengthen and enrich his years. Nothing is so humiliating as to observe the narrow list of themes that interest narrow men.

We were intimately acquainted with a man of good parts who accomplished much in the world. He was so fond of his garden that he would sometimes remain in it till the twilight deepened into the dark, and he would find himself, as he said, grinning over his cabbages so long as he could see them. A gentleman of our acquaintance once exclaimed of one who removed into the country from the nerve-racking experience of town, " Think of a man of his capability descending to raise cabbages! " But it appears that raising cabbages restored poise and enabled the gardener to do better work than before on purely intellectual lines. Do we not often mistake the meaning of intellectual labor? In fact, who can dwell in the realm of pure ideas? Are not all our words originally from the sod, as it were? Does not the spirit come from wind and Psyche mean a soul, which is a breath? How long can any one live on stilts? If a man's head is to be permanently in the clouds, his feet must be permanently on the ground. The most soulful person is also the most human. The modern false suggestion of unreality about life can only lead to a thousand fads and fancies, unsubstantial and vicious. At present we have no use for a soul without a body, because as far as our experience goes up to the present time the use of the soul is to guide a body and use it.

Mr. Edison says that we are composed of an innumerable number of entities. Whether he would say that a man himself was an entity we

NEW HAMPSHIRE HILLS — HANOVER

A CORNER IN CORN — CORNISH

HANOVER HILLS — CONNECTICUT RIVER

GATHERING LILIES — HOPKINTON

NASHUA'S CIVIC CENTER

do not know, but we do know that the finest development of individuality
is that which most nearly co-relates body and mind. We may, indeed, say
that all is mind; or we may say that all is matter. It makes very little
practical difference what names we give to things and manifestations. We
may name a motor a Lizzie or a Jerusalem. What difference, so long as
it only goes? Mr. Edison again thinks that entities, too small ever to be
observed by the microscope, are intelligent. Just consider the inconceiv-
able number of these entities, a figure one followed by a row of ciphers
across a couple of pages at least, and yet altogether making up one indi-

vidual who is afraid to start on a journey on Friday! or another individual who cannot extract the square root of a number! We wish that these intelligent entities were more intelligent. At least, let us give them some sort of a chance in our bodies. We Americans cook our brains and smoke them and suffuse them with certain liquids and then wonder that we produce no more geniuses.

What is sanity? Is it not that necessary capacity of seeing two sides of a question? Is it not the perception that life is dual? Is it not hinged upon a degree of unselfishness? The insane is an absolute egoist. He perhaps became insane by thinking too much of himself or about himself. Had he obeyed the behests of the sanest of Men he would have considered the lilies, how they grow. Knowledge, to begin with, seems to depend very largely upon the comparison of various objects. The man shut in four walls is too limited to be in the class of objects which he may compare. His poetry would lack the lilt of the bard who played on Avon banks. To do one thing supremely it is necessary to do other things a great part of the time. That is to say, the pure specialist consumes himself and runs in a circle and his powers of deduction suffer by the over-development of his powers of observation on one theme. The most interesting life is the one which sees the similes, the analogies, the varieties in the created world. We live in an age of specialties gone mad. A general development of all the powers of a man produces a far more pleasing and valuable character than does the development of a specialist. The slogan of the coming generation should be " General culture." The man who knows only one thing cannot know that very well. We are aware that we are apparently transgressing generally accepted laws when we make such a statement. But in the case of the man who knows one thing well, how can he define that one thing or define its action, its use, its meaning in the world, unless he knows what surrounds his one subject?

CORNISH CLOUDS

INDEX